DEM●S

Demos is an independent think-tank committed to radical thinking on the long-term problems facing the UK and other advanced industrial societies.

It aims to develop the ideas – both theoretical and practical – that will help to shape the politics of the 21st century, and to improve the breadth and quality of political debate.

Demos publishes books and a quarterly journal and undertakes substantial empirical and policy-oriented research projects. Demos is a registered charity.

In all its work Demos brings together people from a wide range of backgrounds in business, academia, government, the voluntary sector and the media to share and cross-fertilise ideas and experiences.

GW00630994

For further information and
subscription details please write to:
Demos
9 Bridewell Place
London, EC4V 6AP
Telephone: 0171 353 4479
Facsimile: 0171 353 4481
email: martin@demos.demon.co.uk

Freedom's Children

Helen Wilkinson and Geoff Mulgan

DEM☉S

First published in 1995 by
Demos
9 Bridewell Place
London EC4V 6AP
Telephone: 0171 353 4479
Facsimile: 0171 353 4481
e-mail martin@demos.demon.co.uk

Paper No. 17
ISBN 1 898309 27 2
Printed in Great Britain by
EG Bond Ltd
Designed by Esterson Lackersteen
Thanks to Adrian Taylor

Contents

Acknowledgements

This report is the culmination of a year long research project which has involved an interim report, a series of working papers and a seminar series. To acknowledge everyone who has contributed to the arguments and project as it has developed would be impossible. However a number deserve special mention.

We are particularly indebted to generous funding from the Joseph Rowntree Charitable Trust. Without their initial support, this project could never have happened. We are also grateful to the representatives of our other funders, in particular Phil Ward, Group Personnel Executive of Northern Foods; David May, Head of Equal Opportunities at NatWest; Victoria Hillier, BT's Development and Training Manager and Jan David, BT's Equal Opportunities Manager; Tony Allen, Human Resources Partner and Susan Hills who works in the Human Resources Division of Coopers & Lybrand; Sandra Sanglin, who was until recently IBM UK's Social Policy Manager and Lesley Holland, Corporate Equality Adviser to the BBC.

We are also grateful to an unusually wide range of academic helpers. Professor Ray Pahl from the University of Essex and a Demos Associate has acted as Helen's academic mentor throughout this project. The authors of the Working Papers also provided crucial inputs. They include: David Cannon from the London Business School, Professor Cary Cooper from Manchester School of Management, Dr Suzan Lewis from Manchester Metropolitan University, Dr Gerda Siann, from Glasgow Caledonian University, Professor Rosemary Crompton, now at the University of Leicester and Professor Angela Coyle from City University. A number of practitioners also contributed working papers: Jane Grant who until recently led the National Alliance of Women's Organisations; Dr Sebastian Kraemer from the Tavistock Clinic; Carol Samms from McCann-Erickson Europe and Viki Cooke and Deborah Mattinson from Opinion Leader Research who were contracted to do qualitative research.

Acknowledgements

Our thanks also extend to Robert Lane, Jeremy Rifkin, Gary Cross, Juliet Schor, Theodore Zeldin, Oliver Sparrow, Jonathon Gershuny and Patricia Hewitt, all of whom contributed to *The time squeeze,* a special issue of the *Demos Quarterly* which formed part of this project.

Special thanks are owed to Nick Winkfield, a Partner at MORI and Managing Director of *Socioconsult* who provided Demos with his analysis of the *Socioconsult* survey, which provides the key source for this report and which is presented here for the first time. Nick went far beyond the call of duty in both providing and analysing the data for us for a nominal fee. Rachel Smith at Essex's Centre for Micro-Social Change provided very helpful advice on making the best use of the British Household Panel Study. Our thanks also extend to Jan Hall, European Chief Executive of Gold Greenlees Trott and a Demos Trustee, who, along with Lady Howe, Chairman of Opportunity 2000, established a link with Forum UK many of whose members gave up their time to fill in an informal questionnaire and to be interviewed on issues relating to the project.

Bob Tyrrell, Chairman of the Henley Centre, gave us permission to draw on their Planning for Social Change programme; Carol Samms of McCann Erickson gave us permission to publish their own research; David Cannon allowed us to publish his extensive qualitative research on young people in Europe and North America and Pat Dade, Director of Synergy Brand Values, gave us permission to draw on their data for the interim report.

Finally, Sarah Gregory and Rebecca Stanley provided invaluable help in the final stages of the project, particularly with footnotes, bibliography and the rather painstaking fact-checking process. Naturally, for all of those who have been involved, the usual disclaimers apply.

Introduction

This report is the culmination of a year-long project which has involved one of the most thorough analyses of a generation's attitudes and experience ever undertaken in the UK. It began with the publication of *No Turning Back: generations and the genderquake* in the autumn of 1994. Since then we have tested the hypotheses set out in that report – primarily concerning the nature and depth of generational shifts in values – through in-depth qualitative and quantitative research. 12 working papers have been published on everything from equal opportunities policy to fathering. A wide body of new research data has been gathered from MORI *Socioconsult* and the ESRC British Household Panel Study at Essex University, as well as many other sources, to test and deepen our understanding of the issues.

This research has overwhelmingly confirmed the depth and extent of change: the rising power of women, the convergence of values between younger men and women, and the rejection of traditional restraints. It has also confirmed that overall this generation believes that life has improved compared to their parent's generation.

But the research has also thrown up many surprises: the attachment to violence amongst younger women, the intense frustration of many working women in the C1 and C2 categories, the rejection of national identity, and the signs of a serious disconnection from society not only amongst groups like single parents, but also in different ways amongst a wider group of young people, both poor and relatively wealthy.

But the core of the book is really about freedom. Most members of this generation take for granted that they can control their own lives, whether in terms of relationships or careers, lifestyles or beliefs. The old assumption that you had to inherit an occupation, a class identity, a religion and a standardised family life has gone for good. But with new freedoms come new problems: how to ensure greater commitments in family life; how to achieve stability in a far more fluid labour market; how to create a sense of common purpose and ownership in the political system; and how to balance autonomy and interdependence.

This is why we have chosen the title 'Freedom's Children'. For the members of this generation are, more than any before them, the inheritors of freedom. They value it deeply. For women in particular there is no support for turning the clock back, to the rigid families and hierarchical workplaces of the past.

But having won the historic battles to achieve freedom, we now have to move on. The book therefore aims to set out some of the elements of the new agenda, striking a balance between a naive libertarianism that can see only the benefits of freedom and none of the costs, and an overly restrictive communitarianism that would seek to deny autonomy and suppress diversity.

Our goal has been to suggest practical ways in which we can achieve a better quality of life for the over seven million men and seven million women now aged between 18 and 34 in Britain today and those who will come after them.

Summary

The values of young people in Britain today have been **profoundly shaped by prosperity** and peace, education, travel and communications, and by an inheritance of freedoms. This generation is the **most educated ever**: 90 per cent of 16-24 year old women have qualifications compared to barely a half of 35-55 year olds. There is a steady shift towards what some commentators call 'post-material' values. Our map of British values also shows how **values are fragmenting**, as younger age groups move towards more 'modern' values, such as autonomy and authenticity . Our survey evidence describes the swing away from tradition and authority, and rising tolerance. Women over 55 are three times as attached to the neighbourhood and traditional values as those under 35. We show how **men's values** are becoming more **feminine** and how **women are becoming more masculine**, attached to risk, hedonism and living on the edge. In particular, women in the youngest age groups are taking far more **pleasure in violence** – more even than young men. 13 per cent of 18-24 year old women agree that 'it is acceptable to use physical force to get something you really want'. We expect female violence to become a major issue in the years ahead.

There are some important class distinctions. C2DE women are now more **committed to achieving success** than their male equivalents, and more frustrated that their ambitions are not being realised. However most of the changes in values are better explained in generational terms, rather than as effects of class or lifestage. In other words, today's young people will probably still hold similar values in middle age. Overall, we find that young people are relatively happy, **more optimistic than older age groups**, and, despite unemployment and negative equity, see their lives as substantially better than those of their parents.

Working life – balancing opportunity and security

This generation is strongly **committed to work**. But the old structures for work have rapidly broken down, with new opportunities and **new insecurities**: half of all job changes now occur before the age of 30 and more than four times as many 16-24 year old men are in temporary jobs as any other age group. Only a third of 16-24 year olds in jobs have a **union at their workplace** and fewer than half of these are members. Women's position has substantially improved – especially for professionals. The typical female professional is now young while the typical male professional is old. The gap on **promotion opportunities** is disappearing for the youngest age group. The proportion of women earning more than their partners has risen from one in fifteen in the early 1980s to one in five today. But there is still a 'family gap' – as women lose their position and pay when having children. Overall this generation has very high – and often unrealistic – expectations of work. Few are at ease with **insecurity**, and there is a strong desire for more balance between work and life – not just for parents but also for single people.

The report recommends a **new deal at work**, above all to restore trust. This requires openness and honesty – even about unpleasant decisions such as redundancies; some long-term commitments to employees, with task flexibility as the quid pro quo, rather than always seeking maximum job flexibility, and willingness to help those whose employment future is uncertain through training schemes.

For employees in small firms there is a need for new strategies which offer a degree of security and stability. A role could be played by TECs forming skills clubs. Others would benefit from a greater role for what we call '**deployers**' – firms which sell their labour but also support them. These could be encouraged through tax policies which reverse the current disincentives against any employer commitment.

For many the key symbol of trust is **training**. Today's young people know that their future depends on skills – preferably transferable ones. But who will provide them with the skills? We found that 65 per cent of 25-34 year olds (in work and out of work), and two-thirds of working women under 35, had not had any training or education in the last 12 months. For the core workers the business responsibility for training remains, and will be an important symbol of commitment. But the general picture for all young employees is that as firms retrench and governments remain fiscally constrained, they will have to **take more responsibility for their own skills**, including being prepared to pay for courses and qualifications themselves.

Much progress has been made in **equal opportunities**. Many companies have introduced targets and family friendly policies, persuaded by the business case that giving women the best chances to develop their full potential is good for competitiveness. However, there is often little incentive to invest in the opportunities of less skilled women workers, or to address the widening pay gap between women, rather than between women and men. Many policies still seem peripheral, and few are integrated into broader career development strategies, or indeed policies for time. Most targets have proven ineffective and unpopular. **The next phase** of equal opportunities will be about moving away from the crude tools of the past towards diversity strategies within which careers can be helped for all groups of employees; measures which target groups (such as part-timers) within which women and ethnic minorities are over represented; and workforce projections as opposed to targets.

Few jobs are **family friendly**. 98 per cent of 25-34 year old women believe employers should help with childcare, but few do. For employers there is a good case for being family friendly, particularly with highly trained staff, and there is now a range of best practice to draw from. But too often such family friendly initiatives are seen as add-ons; they don't impact on the dominant work culture (with its stress on very long hours), or on career development policies. Moreover because they don't usually address the desire for time off of other groups – such as single men – they fail to build wide support. Companies need to move from the model of family friendliness to a broader **work/life** model.

Most firms are still attached to the old idea of a **hierarchical career**. This model fails to take into account obsolescent skills, burnout, midlife crises, and the redundancies (and sideways and downwards shifts) of employees in their fifties. Credible career strategies have to prepare people for **non-linear careers** to fit more varied working patterns; for using time out of work constructively; and for accumulating generic skills rather than the more specific ones that employers tend to prefer. For the employer this may simply require a commitment to time release schemes to enable individuals to train themselves; but larger ones will need to develop career targets (many devised for the individual), strategies for meeting them if they are to be credible, and benchmarks against which progress can be measured.

To achieve greater **choice over time** we argue for lifetime rights to tertiary education combined with income-contingent repayment schemes, rights to unpaid educational leave and rights to parental leave (and rights to reclaiming jobs). We also need **sabbaticals**. In more pressurised and longer lives, we need breaks all the more: opportunities to try out tasks, to learn new skills or even just to have fun. At the moment sabbaticals are an elite luxury. We need to introduce legal backing and a change in attitude.

A large group is becoming steadily **disconnected from work**. Unemployment is running at 21 per cent amongst 16-19 year old men (5 per cent higher than women). Many of the unemployed are cynical not only about the jobs on offer to them, but also about the various training schemes on offer. For these groups it is hard to see how any training schemes, incentives or penalties will get them back in the job market. Although there is a case for subsidising jobs and improving advisory and support services, government will need again to take on its historic role as an **employer of last resort**, through schemes of community service like the Demos CONNECT scheme and also through a parallel scheme of **Community Service for Old People** which can link young people and old in the same projects so as to **avoid stigma**. We also recommend special policies for helping single parents into work. Most credible schemes will entail substantial costs (the idea that getting people into work saves government money is largely an illusion). But the alternative is likely to be a further disconnection from society and its values.

Relationships

It is in relationships and family life that the new costs and benefits of freedom have been felt most acutely. Most people have taken advantage of new freedoms. Only 8.5 per cent of women 16-24 believe that 'a husband should earn and a wife stay at home' compared to almost 63 per cent of women over 55. **Marriage rates have fallen** by a half since the early 1970s. Half of women born in the 1960s have cohabited compared with only 19 per cent born in the 1940s. Most people now **cohabit before marriage** and a third of children are being born outside marriage. 29 per cent of women and 51 per cent of men 18-34 want 'to delay having children as long as possible.' Marriage is being redefined to be **less about economics** and more about intimacy. A more transactional approach is taking root. Once atypical families are spreading, including **single parents** and gay couples. 75.4 per cent of women 16-24 believe that single parents can bring up a child as well as a couple. Within the **household life** is becoming **more equal**. The housekeeping allowance has virtually gone, and the imbalance on household labour (cleaning, cooking etc) looks set to disappear within the next decade: primarily because **young women are accepting male standards of cleanliness** rather than vice-versa.

The biggest costs of the new landscape come from broken relationships. We need to do far more to teach people **how to negotiate relationships** – with skills that may owe more to the boardroom or even war than to romance. We recommend a series of steps to **help cohabiting couples** – access to mediation services, rights to adopt, a new legal opt-out approach to confer rights in the event of relationship breakdown – including access rights for fathers and some financial and property rights. Few are aware of the legal no-man's land they are in.

For parents we propose a **'new parentalism'** which substantially shifts policy towards children, recognising that increasingly men want to be involved more in parenting while women's own well-being depends on being able to mix work and parenting. We propose replacing the married persons tax allowance with allowances targetted to children; rights to parental leave; childcare vouchers that can be spent with close relations such as grandparents as well as formal organisations; allocating to children a share of assets in the case of a divorce or separation; and special training credits for parents who take time off work.

In parallel we need new measures to tackle the **care deficit**, since this generation risks being sandwiched between their children's care needs and those of their parents. The German model of insurance has some virtues but needs to be adapted to ensure that the care burden does not fall solely on women.

Finally we argue **not for abandoning marriage but for modernising it**. As a ceremony marriage remains rigidly constrained. We argue for **deregulation** of marriage to enable people to determine where they marry and to allow a far wider range of 'celebrants' to be registered. Liberalisation would open up exciting new possibilities as well as lowering the cost – which is currently around £8,500 on average.

Reconnecting politics

For this generation **politics has become a dirty word**. Our research finds that they are **less likely to vote, to join a party or to be politically active**. Under 25s are four times less likely to be registered than any other group. In general the young are less active than the old, the poor less than the rich, women less than men, and ethnic minorities less than the white majority.

Similar trends of disconnection are apparent in **other countries**, where they have prompted a far more serious response than in the UK. Political disconnection also leads to a broad social disconnection: just 49 per cent of 18-34 year olds say they would be willing to sacrifice some individual freedom in the public interest compared to 61.5 per cent of 35-54 year olds. Over a third of 18-24 year olds take **pride in being outside the system**. But they are nevertheless concerned about many issues: environment, AIDS, jobs and above all animals. Some analyse their disconnection in terms of contentment. But there are strong signs of discontent: deep-seated distrust of the system, and frustrated ambitions, particularly amongst women. Over half of under 25 year olds register as profoundly disconnected from the system, and a growing number of 'underdogs' are now prepared to bite back – we call them the **underwolves**.

Elsewhere – especially the US – we can see the

beginnings of **intergenerational conflict** over policies and resources. The divide is symbolised by towns which have gleaming new hospitals, run-down schools and impoverished single mothers. Some of the same causes are present in the UK, as this generation faces the prospect of having to pay for old people without the confidence that their own pensions and care needs will be financed. The proportion of women who see pensions as primarily the state's responsibility falls from 55 per cent amongst 35-54 year olds to 43.2 per cent amongst 18-34 year olds.

We call for new measures to reconnect young people and politics. In the first place, reshaping politics with **elections held over a week** or weekend, **polling stations** in places like **shopping centres**, and far more **active registration** initiatives linked to driving licences, banks and other bodies (one in five 21-24 year olds is not registered). We also argue for a system of **required voting** for national elections and referendums – following the Australian model – whereby failure to vote would result in a small fine. We recommend this on the grounds that it is better to accept a small infringement of freedom every few years, than to accept that a large proportion of the population will become wholly disconnected from politics and power. **New technologies** also need to be used: 70 per cent of 18-34 year olds are keen to use TVs, telephones and computers to vote at elections.

But we also need a new intergenerational deal . In part this will mean a **new balance in spending** and a shift to **intergenerational accounting** – accounting public programmes in terms of the costs and benefits for each generation so as to promote greater clarity and long-termism. Politicians also need to come clean about the real prospects for this generation. At present **half of this generation is not saving**. Given the fiscal limits, and the limits of existing incentives, if many are to avoid serious poverty in old age they will depend on a shift to compulsory saving schemes.

The central argument is that **freedom's children** need a

new set of frameworks to define life in work, in relationships and in politics. New freedoms have brought far richer life opportunities, especially for women. No-one wants to give these away. But the hard task now is to define a sustainable framework for freedoms, and a better balance between choice and commitment.

The fracturing of British values

The importance of understanding values should be self-evident. They frame the operating environment for politics and business, and for institutions from schools to police forces. They can determine whether societies feel united or divided, happy or unhappy.

The values of the 18-34 year old generation are distinctive from previous generations. Whereas previous generations were formed by such things as the 1930s depression and the second world war, this generation has been shaped by an inheritance of unprecedented freedoms: the freedoms of social mobility and education, freedom for women to work and to control their own reproduction, and freedom to define one's own lifestyle. As we shall see this inheritance is reflected in a spirit of optimism, a strong belief in autonomy, and a genuine relief at the disappearance of the rigid rules that governed their parents and grandparents.

But as this report makes clear, the story is more complex. Greater freedom is being paralleled by a crisis of trust. Many have lost faith in politics and authority more generally. Others are disillusioned because, compared to the rising living standards, full employment and generous welfare provision of previous generations, they are now suffering from negative equity, job insecurity and unemployment. Moreover, greater freedom, openness, generosity and tolerance within this generation can be found alongside signs of a narrow, selfish individualism and, for a minority, of a more profound disconnection from society as a whole.

How possible is it to make any firm assertions about how values are changing? How confident can we be about the conclusions that are drawn? Most reasonably educated people assume that although things like demography and economics are knowable and predictable, values must be ephemeral, unmeasurable, subject to whims and fashions. They are 'soft' and should be always discounted relative to the 'hard' data of money flows or physical materials. Surprisingly, however, there is now abundant evidence that values often change steadily, and to a degree, predictably, and if, as in this report, values are consistently checked against the harder evidence of behaviour, we have good reason to take them seriously.

Probably the world's most thorough and original researcher of changing values is Ronald Inglehart, who has used the huge body of data collected for the European Values group, and more recently the World Values survey, to analyse how values change.[1] His central conclusion is that as a result of long term economic security (mainly since world war two), there has been a major inter-generational shift from 'materialist' to 'post-materialist' values, that is an increased emphasis upon quality of life issues rather than money or social order. The argument draws directly on Abraham Maslow's famous hierarchy of human need – which suggested that satisfaction of basic needs would be followed by a greater interest in the higher needs of self-fulfilment and spirituality. Barring a catastrophic economic downturn or a major war, Inglehart argues, these changes are likely to persist. He writes: "The change is gradual. It reflects changes in the formative experiences that have shaped different generations....As younger generations gradually replace older ones in the adult population, the prevailing world view of these societies is being transformed." [2]

His book *Culture Shift in Advanced Industrial Society* gathered a wide range of evidence to confirm his thesis. The table overleaf sets out the data for a number of European countries and shows the clear pattern – the steady shift to postmaterial values, and the sharp downturns in periods of economic crisis.

Inglehart's ideas have generated intensive debate. But by and large they have been confirmed, despite valid criticisms of methodologies and interpretations. Much of his argument is also borne out by our research, although in our view there are problems with both his definitions (his definition of post-materialism for example is often closer to other people's definition of libertarianism) and his causal argument (for example, he is probably wrong to think that adherence to post-material values necessarily implies a rejection of material ones; young people may increasingly want their work to give them both fulfilment and high pay). But the core argument about generational formation and values has largely been confirmed: although individuals do change their attitudes and values over time, generations have distinctive clusters of values which they take with them through their lives.

Fragmenting values

How then does this help us understand values in Britain? Some of the implications are fairly clear – for example, any return to strong growth and a sense of economic security will probably push green issues high up the political agenda again. But Britain is not an homogeneous society, and the new values of younger generations remain in a minority.

Indeed, as MORI *Socioconsult*'s work for Demos shows, British values are now undergoing a marked fragmentation. The map on page 24 shows the clusters

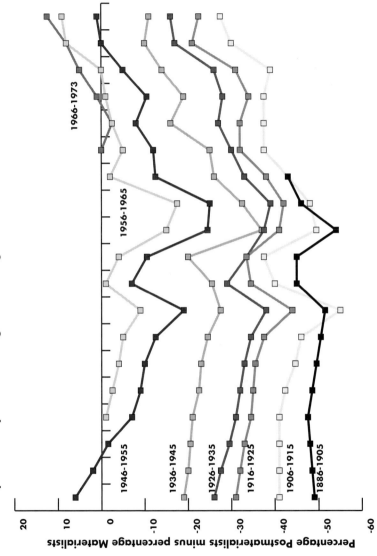

The predictability of value change across the generations

Percentage Postmaterialists minus percentage Materialists

20 10 0 -10 -20 -30 -40 -50 -60

1966-1973
1956-1965
1946-1955
1936-1945
1926-1935
1916-1925
1906-1915
1886-1905

1970 1971 1972 1973 1974 1975 1976 1977 1978 1979 1980 1981 1982 1983 1984 1985 1986 1987 1988

Source: Inglehart, Culture Shift (1990) Based on data from 6 West European countries

23

The fracturing of British values

	BASIC ORIENTATION: TRADITIONAL 'To Preserve'	BASIC ORIENTATION: MATERIALIST 'To have'	CHANGING VALUES		
			HEDONISM 'To indulge'	POST-MATERIALIST 'To be'	POST-MODERN 'To have, to be and to indulge'
Upper	Upper Middle Class Milieu 7%				
Upper middle	Traditional Middle Class Milieu 20%			Progressive Middle Class Milieu 10%	Thatcher's Children 4%
Middle middle		Social Climbers 5%		Socially Concerned 9%	
Lower middle	Traditional Working Class Milieu 21%	Progressive Working Class Milieu 15%			
Lower		British Poor 9%			

▨ = Mileux in which18-34 year olds predominate

Source: Socioconsult

of values on two axes: one is income, or rather socio-economic level, the second maps the 'modernity' of people's values, that is to say the extent to which their values have moved away from traditional ones.

The map shows just how much values are fragmenting. Whereas a few generations ago the values would have clustered closely together, they now range from the traditional upper middle-class, middle and working-class, through to 'Thatcher's Children' (the usually highly educated young who are concerned with material success and the pursuit of pleasure), the 'social climbers' (usually people from working class backgrounds who are building careers), and the socially concerned in the public sector and caring professions. The map is also a snapshot of generational change. Whereas older age groups predominate on the lefthand side of the map, younger people tend to be on the righthand side, more strongly attached to autonomy.

It is not hard to see how many problems this map throws up for employers or political parties. As values fragment (and MORI *Socioconsult* expect more discrete milieux to emerge during the second half of the 1990s) it is becoming ever harder to appeal to everyone. At the same time although the demographic majority is still on the left of this map (and so long as young people don't bother to vote this skew is accentuated in the political market), the future trend seems to be away from these values and towards the modern and post-modern values.

The drivers of change

Why is this happening? What are the key drivers of change for this generation? Previous values analysis across the Western world has tended to emphasise such things as communications and travel, education and economic prosperity. It is these that transform people's horizons, their sense of possibility. This generation certainly has access to far cheaper communication and media than its predecessors. Europeans aged 15-24, for example, are already almost as likely to have visited another European country as those over 25, and the proportion of Europeans who can speak more than two languages has risen from 28 per cent in 1969 to 42 per cent in 1990.[3] New technologies are also having an obvious impact: many of the 200-300,000 Internet users in the UK fall within the age group.[4]

As we shall see changing gender roles have also been a massive force for change, undermining traditional values, and perceptions of work and family. Their momentum shows no signs of diminishing, not least because of the effects of education. The young – particularly women – are now considerably more educated (at least in terms of qualifications) than any previous generation as the table below shows. Over 90 per cent of 16-24 year old women have some level of academic qualification, and they have the highest proportion of A and O levels. 25-34 year olds are more likely to have higher degrees, for obvious reasons, but we can expect their successors to outstrip them. By contrast, nearly half of women aged between 35-55 have no academic qualifications at all.

Women's highest academic qualification (%)

	Age			
	16-24	25-34	35-55	56yrs+
Higher degree	9.0	18.2	14.2	6.6
A Level	26.4	15.7	9.2	3.3
O Level	42.2	37.5	28.7	11.4
CSE	13.0	13.9	2.3	0.1
None of these	9.4	14.7	45.6	78.7

Source: British Household Panel Study (Base, 4562)

This escalation of qualifications brings much in its wake: a greater desire to translate educational achievements into success at work; a greater assumption of autonomy and the capacity to make choices.

It gives people the confidence to stand on their own two feet – explaining why, for example, 69 per cent of men and 43 per cent of women in the 18-24 age band would rather be self-employed entrepreneurs than 9-5 employees. In later chapters we analyse in much greater detail how these various drivers are interacting with relationships and the home, with work and politics. But the crucial point at this stage is that most of the obvious driving forces on values are accelerating, not slowing down.

Generational values

What then are the specific trends happening in terms of the values of the 18-34 year old age group? Across a range of dimensions we have gathered evidence of pulling apart, a growing gap in values between the generations.

The graph overleaf provides a snapshot of some of the biggest gaps in values between the generations. These can be found on issues such as the 'flexible family' – belief in the rights of both partners in a relationship, and their children, to do their own thing. This is very much a new value, strong amongst the youngest age groups. We can also see the rising importance of authenticity – the search for relationships that are honest and straightforward, and possessions that convey meaning rather than status. And we can see the rise of attachment to what we term 'techno-nature', the combination of green beliefs and confidence that new technologies can help solve the problems of the environment.

There are also marked gaps in attitudes to living. We can see the strong attachment amongst the young to living life on the edge, to taking risks and to hedonism. In many cases (and this has been confirmed by our qualitative research) the gap seems to be accelerating at the younger end of the age group, with a deepening of individualism. But these are not the only values which show marked generational differences. In what follows we map out in more detail the key shifts in values, distinguishing those that are likely to be ephemeral from those that have a longer term significance.

Values and age: attachment index

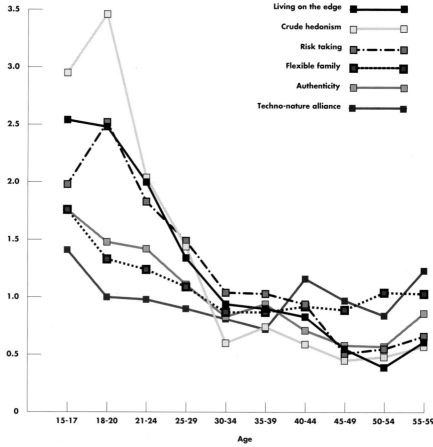

Living on the edge
Crude hedonism
Risk taking
Flexible family
Authenticity
Techno-nature alliance

Source: Socioconsult (Base, 1651)

The swing away from tradition

The first shift is the weakening of tradition, whether in the form of deference to authority, adherence to rigid moral codes of right and wrong behaviour, or attachments to community and the family.[5] Our *Socioconsult* analysis shows wide gulfs in values between the generations. Amongst women, those over 55 are roughly three times as attached to the neighbourhood and to traditional values, and nearly twice as attached to national chauvinism as 18-34 year olds. Amongst men, attachments to neighbourhood and tradition also fall steadily with each generation.

Religion is a good example of how many traditional values are not being passed on. 83 per cent of people aged between 18-34 have a Christian background but only 58 per cent say they practise or believe and whilst only 9 per cent have an atheist background, 27 per cent consider themselves to be atheist. As many as 61 per cent agree that people should be allowed to do anything they want so long as it doesn't harm anyone else, and 48 per cent that moral rights and wrongs should be decided by the majority of people in society; only 14 per cent agree that 'what the Church says about what is morally right or wrong has a strong influence on my life'. Most can recall only two or three of the Ten Commandments.[6] This is also true of ethnic minorities; one recent qualitative study found that attachment to religion, strong amongst the first generation, is considerably weaker amongst their children.[7]

The swing away from authority

There are also signs of a shift from an essentially authoritarian to a liberal culture. The latest British Social Attitudes report[8] found that 63 per cent of adults over 60 years of age have a broadly 'authoritarian' world view compared to 27 per cent of 18-34 year olds. Older people are twice as likely as younger people to hold authoritarian views with more censorious views of unconventional behaviour.

29

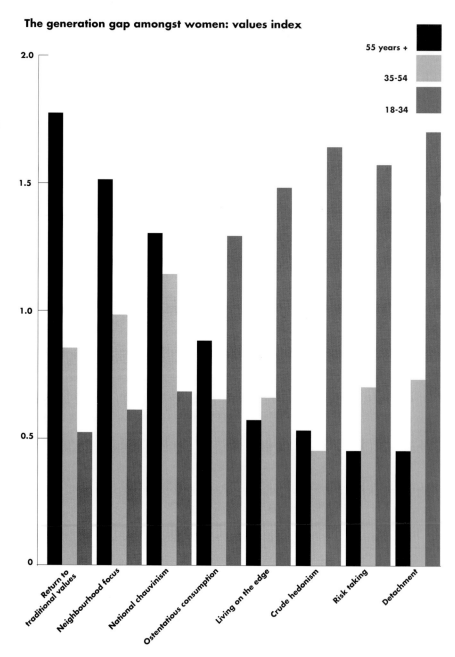

The fracturing of British values

The generation gap amongst women: values index

55 years +

35-54

18-34

2.0

1.5

1.0

0.5

0

Return to traditional values
Neighbourhood focus
National chauvinism
Ostentatious consumption
Living on the edge
Crude hedonism
Risk taking
Detachment

Source: Socioconsult (Base, 1102)

This is not to say that young people are tolerant of crime or violence; many hold permissive views on personal morality combined with tough views on law and order. It is rather that the general trend is towards more libertarian tolerance for morally debatable acts and religious orientation.

There are many who see this simply as a natural feature of youth and assume that as people become older they become less tolerant.

But longitudinal research in Europe suggests that "the differences between age groups in levels of tolerance arise not because people become less tolerant as they grow older but because over the second half of the century, each successive European generation has been more tolerant than the previous one".[9]

The swing away from traditional masculinity
The move away from tradition has also brought a 'feminisation' of men's values.[10] This can be explained in part by the disappearance of traditional male roles in the army, in manufacturing and construction. In *No Turning Back*: *generations and the genderquake* we showed that women are leading the overall patterns of change in British values and our *Socioconsult* data confirms this, showing that younger men are becoming much more attached to what might be seen as 'soft' and 'caring' values, and those that confront 'male logic', ie a left-brained perspective, with the right-brained 'female logic' or intuition.

Women are considerably more attached than men to these 'feminine' values in the over-55 age group; in all of the middle groups the gender gap is closing and by the time we reach the 18-34 age range young men match young women on what might have been thought to be typically feminine values. As we shall see these values are changing attitudes to parenting (where younger men want more involvement), to caring jobs, and to intimacy and emotional honesty.

The masculinisation of young women

The feminising of men is being matched by the masculinisation of women. The table below shows just how much younger women are becoming attached to more 'masculine' values.

Masculine values index

Value	Sex	Age		
		15-17	*18-34*	*35-54*
Crude hedonism				
	female	3.83	1.64	0.45
	male	2.28	1.58	0.67
Seeking success				
	female	2.44	1.06	0.85
	male	1.91	1.18	0.71
Risk taking				
	female	2.91	1.57	0.70
	male	1.38	1.58	0.84

Source: Socioconsult (Base, 1511)

Risk taking is a good example; many more young women seem to enjoy doing things that are physically dangerous or forbidden. Parachute jumps for charity and bungie jumping have as much appeal to young women as to young men. The attachment to risk also means that younger women are more likely to set themselves up in business. Women aged between 35-54 by contrast are attached to many of the caring values that we might expect: they have a traditional/conservative rather than a modern/experimental orientation, and they are well below the total population average on more individualistic values.

Similarly the value 'crude hedonism' (which is about enjoying life today, doing things for the thrill, and leading as full a life as possible) appeals to young women much more than old. We find a similar trend with 'living on the edge'. Younger women are considerably more attached to this value than older generations of women. 53 per cent of 18-24 year old women agree that 'from time to time I like to do things that are dangerous'.

Perhaps the most disturbing trend is the darker side of this attraction to masculine values. While it might be less surprising that 25 per cent of young men aged 18-24 agree that 'it's acceptable to use physical violence to get something you want' our data also shows a remarkable rise in attachment to violence amongst younger women, with 13 per cent of 18-24 year old women agreeing. We are already hearing of growing numbers of girl gangs and criminals. The figures below, which show young girls overtaking boys in their attachment to violence, suggest it could become an epidemic:

Pleasure in violence index

Sex	Age		
	15-17	18-34	35-54
female	3.35	1.36	0.55
male	2.49	1.45	0.61

Source: Socioconsult (Base, 1511)

Transient values, lifestage and class

These changing values – and other ones such as attitudes to pre-marital sex or animal rights –look profound, and look to be deepening. But it is vital to know which of these shifts are irreversible and which are transient. Critics of values research and analyses of cohort or generational effects tend to emphasise the way in which people's values change as they age. The critical variable, they argue, is not which generation you belong to but what stage you are at in your life.

For them a 'generation gap' is a natural effect of different lifestages, and apparent value shifts are transient. Thus recent research on the attitudes and values of today's youth (those under 25) which finds that as many as three in ten want to be as different as possible from their parents does not seem terribly surprising.[11] The journalists and cynics quite rightly ask: 'wasn't it ever thus?' Moreover there is certainly a good body of evidence which suggests that some attitudes do change with age – for example the advent of a family often leads to less egalitarian behaviour and attitudes.

Clearly it is crucial to distinguish permanent from temporary changes. There is a big difference between *period effects*, when the whole of society is affected by events or by a change in culture (for example World War Two or the 1960s); *lifestage effects*, when different attitudes can be explained by people's lifestage – (for example whether they have children) and *generational effects*, when each successive generation has a somewhat different body of values which change cumulatively (for example deference or adherence to traditional moral codes). Fortunately there are a number of tools for distinguishing these:

● we can examine how attitudes at different ages change over time with longitudinal data from various countries to map out the picture of a 'culture shift' (see the table on page 24 which shows the surprising stability of each generation's values as they age)
● we can examine how particular changes in how people live (eg having children or getting married) affect their values

Our own data shows that some values do indeed change. There are fairly consistent patterns which seem to be linked to lifestage. After 18, a typical age for leaving home, many young men and women particularly enjoy taking risks, having fun and living on the edge. In the mid twenties, as more people form lasting relationships and settle down, attachment to these values declines and more energies are devoted to consumption. But most values appear to be unaffected by lifestage, and for those that are – hedonism is a good example – the patterns are more interesting than one might expect. From our own survey, as the table below shows, it would seem that for women the greatest shifts come when a relationship is formed whereas for men they come when children are born. Once the family is established, the gender gap appears to close once again.[12]

34

Crude hedonism index

	Men	Women	Difference
Young singles	2.44	3.29	+0.85
Newly weds	1.98	1.43	-0.55
Young family	0.90	1.13	+0.23
Middle aged family	0.61	0.61	Zero

Source: Socioconsult (Base ,688

The key group which seems to buck these trends are single parents. Their values show little signs of being 'tamed' by the fact of parenthood. This may be because they are more alienated than other groups in society. 56 per cent of single mothers are not satisfied with their lives, but see it as the best they can hope for. 14 per cent see it as 'acceptable to use physical force to get something you really want', and 48 per cent believe 'it will always be impossible to reform the system...we need to close it down and start again'. Their detachment is a.subject to which we return in more depth later.

Class and generation

If one main criticism of values analysis is that it ignores lifestage, the other is that it downplays class. Most opinion polls still use occupational definitions as their primary means of breaking the population down (hence the focus of political strategists on groups like the 'C2s'). And many like to believe that values directly follow from one's socioeconomic position.

In fact the patterns of values are far more complex. Casual observers often claim that the changes in generational values are confined to the wealthy and higher educated, and are therefore not relevant to society as a whole. In fact there is a remarkable degree of consistency across the class range. Although there are class differences – overall ABC1 men are more 'feminine' and ABC1 women more 'masculine', many values – the rejection of tradition, more libertarian values and behaviours – have spread to all classes. This is particularly true of women: the idea that feminist values are still the preserve of the higher educated middle class is simply not true.

Attitudes to success are a good indicator of how class, generation and gender are intersecting. Although ABC1 men are still slightly more driven than their female counterparts, amongst C2DEs the opposite is the case: today it is the women who are most attached to success, a remarkable historic turnaround.

Seeking success index (18-34 year olds)

Sex	Index	
	ABC1	C2DE
Women	.83	1.11
Men	1.06	0.94

Source: Socioconsult (Base, 715)

Interestingly the same pattern can be found on other values – such as risk, hedonism and violence – with both ABC1 men and C2DE women most strongly attached.

But the more striking class gap is on 'frustrated ambition'. As life expectations have risen throughout society, those with fewer opportunities are becoming increasingly dissatisfied with their lives and increasingly certain that there is something standing in their way.

Frustrated ambition index (18-34 year olds)

Sex	Index	
	ABC1	C2DE
Women	0.55	1.30
Men	0.73	1.27

Source: Socioconsult (Base, 715)

A closing of the generation gap?

This chapter has mapped a complex picture of values. It has shown a series of possibly widening gulfs – on morality and behaviour, on violence and aspiration. It has provided some of the grounds for expecting that the map of values, presented at the beginning, will continue to fragment, rendering Britain in all probability a nation less at ease with itself.

Yet there is for all that one reason to be hopeful. Although there are significant differences between the young and the middle aged, the starkest generation gap is with women and men aged over 55. Each subsequent generation has become more tolerant, and more attached to autonomy and personal fulfilment. The implication is that in the long-run the generation gap may narrow rather than widen.

Certainly there is some evidence of more tolerance between the generations. One study recently found that in 15 of 16 countries in Europe a higher proportion of people held favourable attitudes to the young (people under the age of 25) in 1990 than in 1969.[13] Perhaps the sea change in values which led in the direction of secularism, tolerance, and libertarianism in the 1960s is consolidating, while the traditional values of older generations will die with them.

It is also reassuring to find how positively men and women in all classes feel about their own lives in comparison to their parents'. Although it has become common for parents to say that they are the first generation in living memory to expect their children to be worse off than them, roughly 80 per cent of 18-34 year olds are generally optimistic about the future (more than any older age group). Their general satisfaction applies to values, to material possessions, to the relationships between men and women and, crucially, to freedom.

Their optimism is a good antidote to fashionable pessimism. But it is hard to be wholly sanguine. Great progress has been made, but as always new problems come in its wake. Alongside greater freedoms, the overall pattern of fragmenting values may be making British society less cohesive, more divided, and more selfish. In the next chapters we therefore analyse in depth precisely what this may mean in work, relationships and politics.

Working life: balancing opportunity and security

Older people throughout history have portrayed the young as workshy. It would be hard to do so today. Work has become hugely important to the generation under 35, for women as well as men, and our analysis of the British Household Panel Study finds that the young tend to work just as hard as the old, with young professional women now the hardest workers of all.

But the world of work which young people are entering is changing fast. Much of the old order – from apprenticeships to jobs to life – is disintegrating and young people are at the frontline both of the new opportunities and of the new insecurity. While women now have unprecedented chances to build a career, and while the rise of information technologies gives huge advantages to the computer literate young, the other side of the equation is that work has become less certain. Half of all job changes occur before the age of 30 and a quarter before the age of 20,[1] and our analysis of the BHPS finds that the proportion of 16-24 year old men in temporary jobs is more than four times as high as 25-55 year olds, and men born in the 1960s are twice as likely to be self-employed as men born in the 1940s.[2]

The result is that for this generation there are few

guidelines to help them define their relationships to work. Should they be loyal or should they always move if offered a better job? Should they rely on an occupational pension? Should they embrace the fluidity of the modern labour market or seek security?

The individualised workplace

The world of work is fast changing from an industrial to a post-industrial order, based around maximum flexibility, information flows, contingent relationships, and personalised rather than collective arrangements.[3] The promise of this model fits the values of this generation well because it promises much greater autonomy. Optimistic management gurus such as William Bridges in his book, *Job Shift*[4] argue that we are heading towards a just-in-time workforce headed by self sufficient 'vendor' employees. Work, he and others argue, is being refashioned, as operational decisions are devolved downwards, sometimes even to the home, and as more democratic and open teams introduce a new output-oriented culture hostile to hierarchy and the glass ceiling. Much the same analysis can be found in the writings of Tom Peters, John Naisbitt, Alvin Toffler and Rosabeth Moss Kanter.

According to this analysis, people will have relationships with many smaller firms rather than a single large company or institution. The focus of career development will move from the organisation to the individual.[5]

Certainly many of the visible labour market trends point in this direction: the decline in full-time jobs, the growth in self-employment and part-time work, the fact that the proportion of white collar workers on temporary contracts has doubled in the last five years to almost one in ten.[6] Many organisations are moving to a model based on a core of permanent staff and a larger periphery of casualised work in many different types of job, ranging from consultants to cleaners. Only 47 per cent of firms expect to keep 90 per cent of their

39

workforce as core employees over the next four years.[7]

Such dramatic changes are having major effects. One is growing variability in pay. Two out of five full-time employees already receive a significant proportion of their annual pay in the form of variable, discretionary bonuses.[8] Another is the further decline in the place of trade unions:[9] our analysis shows that only a third of men and women in employment aged between 16-24 actually have a union at their workplace and fewer than half of these (just 42 per cent) are members. A third effect is rapidly growing flexibility both in working hours (for example 60 per cent of men and 45 per cent of women usually or sometimes work on Saturdays) and in work arrangements: shift working is spreading from the emergency services and manufacturing to many offices and computer firms. 12 per cent of employees now work flexi-time, 9 per cent work annualized hours and 5 per cent work term time only (notably at banks like NatWest).[10] Telework, though marginal, is spreading not only for consultants and journalists but also for secretarial and data entry workers.

Some forecasts of the end of the job for life have been wildly exaggerated, but a recent report, *Lifetime Jobs and Transient Jobs: Job Tenure in Britain, 1975-1992*[11] found mean job tenure down from 10.5 years in 1975 to 9.4 in 1991, and a rapid fall in the proportion of men holding jobs for five years or more (down from 62 per cent in 1984 to 54 per cent in 1991). The authors write "the 18-25 year age group [are] dramatically over-represented in the insecure end of the jobs market". Another report found that job tenure has fallen by 14 per cent since 1975 and that the jobs available to the unemployed are becoming increasingly unstable and low-paid, so that many now face a lifetime of short periods of work and frequent periods of unemployment.[12] Certainly unemployment has become a fact of life, and is higher amongst young people aged between 16-24 than any other age group, with men almost 6 per cent more likely to be unemployed than women.[13] Even higher education is no longer a guarantee of a job; UK graduate unemployment rose to 14.5 per cent in 1993.[14]

The feminisation of work

The old structures of work which are now unravelling were predominantly designed for men.[15] Their demise has brought new opportunities for women. Women now make up almost half the workforce,[16] aided amongst other things by education. According to as yet unpublished research women's relative lack of education has now almost disappeared as a factor shaping women's relative pay and job opportunities,[17] and there has been a dramatic closing of the pay gap for younger more educated women.[18]

Many feminist commentators[19] have challenged the claim that this constitutes progress. Women continue to predominate in low paid and part-time jobs. The title of a recent report, *Plus ca Change* captures their mood.[20] 82 per cent of part-timers and 54 per cent of temporary employees are women[21] and 50 per cent of British mothers working part-time are in the 3 lowest occupational categories, with only 10 per cent in the top 3. In France by contrast, 22.5 per cent of mothers working part-time are in the top 3 categories and only 30 per cent are in the lowest.[22]

The critics argue that in the UK any shift to female preponderance in a job will lead to its status and pay being downgraded (teaching is a classic example),[23] and they point to the growing pay gap between part-time workers and full-time workers[24] which is widening inequality between women.[25]

But it would be wrong simply to accept these arguments as the whole story. In important areas of the workforce women's advance looks irreversible, most visibly perhaps in the professions. The proportion of professionals has increased from 0.6 per cent amongst the mothers of today's 25-34 year olds to 3.9 per cent of their daughters, and there are already more professional women under 35 – 58 per cent – than over. As the table below shows, the typical professional woman is young whereas the typical professional man is old – indeed there are now more female solicitors under 30 than men[26] (and there are, as yet, no signs of lawyers losing their status).

Women and men's jobs (%)

Job description	Age			
	16-24	25-34	35-55	56yrs+
Professional occupation				
Men	2.1	7.5	9.9	10.2
Women	1.9	3.9	1.8	0.8
Managerial and technical				
Men	12.7	30.6	36.5	25.5
Women	11.9	33.4	31.7	24.4
Skilled non-manual				
Men	22.3	14.3	10.1	11.8
Women	48.9	37.7	33.9	32.9
Skilled manual				
Men	30.0	31.5	30.9	32.1
Women	8.7	8.3	8.8	8.5
Partly skilled				
Men	23.3	14.2	10.0	16.2
Women	25.3	13.0	17.4	14.8
Unskilled				
Men	9.6	1.8	2.7	4.2
Women	3.3	3.7	6.4	18.6

Source: British Household Panel Study (Base, 5159)

Nor is this gender shift likely to reverse. Our BHPS analysis shows that the overall gender gap in promotion opportunities which is quite wide in the older age group – 35-55 year olds – standing at about 22 per cent, has narrowed to 6 per cent amongst 25-34 year olds and almost zero (0.4 per cent) amongst 16-24 year olds. Interestingly, too, the number of women earning more than their partners has trebled from 1 in 15 in the early 1980s to 1 in 5 in 1995.[27]

These advances by women are being matched by growing signs that men are having to compete for what were once seen as women's jobs, particularly in areas of high unemployment. 42.5 per cent of men working part-time are now doing so because they cannot find a full time job.[28] Increasingly men of all ages are appearing in service industries and female-dominated manufacturing jobs. Our analysis shows that the younger you are the less likely you are to work in an exclusively female environment; the proportion of women working in jobs where there are roughly equal numbers of men and women rises from 21.5 per cent in the over 56 age group, to 34.7 per cent in the 16-24 age range, while the proportion of men working in exclusively male environments has fallen from roughly a half to barely a third.[29] One effect of this may be to stop the erosion of the relative pay of what were once women's occupations (the catering industry is sometimes cited as an example),[30] since men tend to bargain harder for higher wages.

Our analysis of the BHPS shows that the pay gap has all but disappeared for the youngest women, and stands at 4.3 per cent for 16-24 year olds compared to 50 per cent for 35-55 year olds. But despite this progress there are still important barriers to full equality at work. Above all, the family gap – the pay gap that tends to appear when women have children[31] – has not disappeared.

The ratio of women's earnings relative to men's falls from 82 per cent at the age of 23 for a young single women to 71 per cent for women at the age of 33 and whilst childless women at 33 are just about keeping pace with their male peers, working mothers of the same age earn just 64 per cent as much as men.[32] Moreover working mothers who don't take maternity leave are more likely to suffer from the family gap than women who take job protected maternity leave.[33]

The implication is that contract workers are likely to suffer adversely relative to permanent workers. And whilst many young women are making major advances, the pay gap amongst young women who are less skilled and less educated remains significant.[34]

How values and attitudes are responding to change

How is the 18-34 year old generation coping with these changes? The commitment to work is not in doubt:[35] 78 per cent of 25-34 year olds today would continue to work even if there was no financial need compared to 66 per cent of 45-54 year olds.[36] But is work a source of anything more than income?

Demands and frustrations
Certainly the commitment to work has made people far more demanding. We found that 37 per cent of women and 46 per cent of men in work in the age group say they are looking for a job which 'gives their life meaning'. David Cannon, author of *Generation X and the New Work Ethic*[37] argues that in North America and Europe today's young graduates want work which is interesting as well as well paid, and frequently prefer to work for organisations which offer them autonomy and project based work rather than simply a role in a hierarchical career structure.[38] Surveys of young people in Europe have consistently shown that they want work that is interesting and demanding, and which involves achievement, responsibility and initiative, as well as good pay.[39] There has also been a shift towards more individualistic attitudes to work, including a growing preference for performance related pay.[40] Our own detailed qualitative research[41] – some inside companies, some with representative samples of the public – has confirmed the general findings and shown that even unskilled young workers support performance related pay.[42]

The aspirations to better jobs are widespread.[43] Interestingly, while men continue to demand more from their jobs than women, younger women are rapidly closing the gap. Amongst single women 18-34, 55 per cent want management responsibility and 67 per cent seek 'great possibilities for advancement'.[44] Indeed, on certain issues – for example work as a source of meaning, 15-17 year old women far outstrip the men.

The problem however is a mismatch between aspirations and real opportunities.[45] The tables below show that few people actually get what they want from their job.

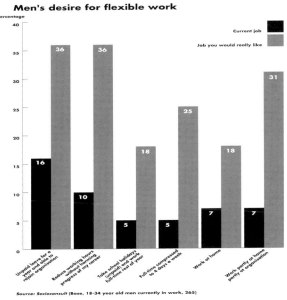

Men's desire for flexible work

Source: Socioconsult (Base, 18-34 year old men currently in work, 265)

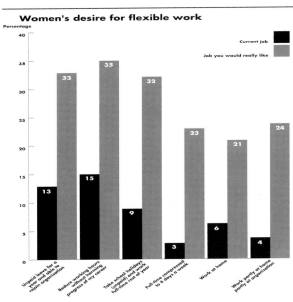

Women's desire for flexible work

Source: Socioconsult (Base, 18-34 year old women currently in work, 194)

Many of these frustrations look set to worsen. Our analysis of the BHPS shows that despite rising aspirations, roughly half of 16-24 year olds, and 42 per cent of 25-34 year olds, report having no promotion opportunities in their current jobs. Predictably this mismatch is likely to be heightened lower down the class scale. Perhaps we shouldn't be surprised that in our *Socioconsult* survey C2DE women are more than twice as likely to feel that their ambitions have been thwarted as ABC1 women.[46] These frustrations may increase in the future as people at the lower end of the age range enter the jobs market and find that many of the jobs likely to be created over the next few decades will remain fairly low skill, and probably fairly low satisfaction.[47]

Coping in the feminised workplace
The good news is that in most respects young people are at ease with the movement of women into work.[48] The table below shows just how much attitudes have changed: only 12.5 per cent of men aged between 16-24 agree that 'A husband should earn and a woman should stay at home' compared to 74.4 per cent of men aged over 55.[49] Amongst women the shift in attitudes is even more dramatic: just 8.3 per cent of 16-24 year olds agree compared to 61.6 per cent of women over 55.

Response to statement 'A husband should earn and a wife should stay at home' (%)

		Age			
		16-24	25-34	35-55	56yrs+
Agree	Women	8.4	11.1	18.1	62.9
	Men	12.5	15.7	28.5	74.4
Disagree	Women	91.6	88.9	81.9	37.1
	Men	87.5	84.3	71.5	25.6

Source: *British Household Panel Study* (Base, 6768)

Yet this picture is not wholly consistent. Many women still feel that they do not get the respect or opportunities at work they deserve. Equal opportunities policies have not filtered down to workers on the shopfloor. Many men – especially those who are less educated – still hold traditional attitudes to 'women's work' and 'men's work' (partly understandably given that women's jobs are still lower paid),[50] although growing numbers are coming to terms with the jobs on offer.

One explanation is simply that recent changes in work are hurting men more than women. Women aged between 18-34 are significantly less likely than men of the same age to say that changes in work are causing them stress, damaging their family life or 'making their life a misery' (30 per cent of C2DE men say that this is the case compared to 15 per cent of women.)[51]

Insecurity
We have found that few young people are at ease with the new insecurities – job security is highly sought after amongst 18-34 year olds in work[52] (50 per cent of women and 60 per cent of men see it as an important characteristic of jobs they want) – partly because, as our analysis of the BHPS shows, young people suffer most from insecurity, short-term contracts and temporary jobs.

Moreover despite a slight trend, our *Socioconsult* analysis shows that younger workers are not happy with having several employers or work activities (if anything it is the C2DEs who wish to have several employers and activities, perhaps to break the monotony of routine work).[53] Few want to become portfolio workers and most seem to want varied and interesting work within organisations (whether large or small) rather than the unpredictability of having to negotiate with many different employers.[54]

Finding balance
While many young people are throwing all their energies into work, *Socioconsult* finds that a significant minority, perhaps up to a quarter of the entire workforce, are deprioritising work. The combination of ever longer working hours and ever less security is

leading people to seek security in relationships and family life.[55]

There are also indications that young people want to get a better balance between work and life, not least because of the 'time squeeze', the combined pressures on time from rising working hours and more time needed for leisure, travel, shopping and childcare.[56] According to *Socioconsult* over 80 per cent of mothers and 88 per cent of fathers aged between 18-34 say they want to spend more time with their family.[57]

As the tables on the next page show, part of the problem is the serious mismatch between the time patterns of the work people want and the work they do.

A sizeable minority of this age group would like to reduce their working hours. While working hours have gone up generally over the last decade, they have gone up particularly for some groups. For example our analysis of the BHPS finds that professional women under 24 work the longest hours of any occupation and any age group: 7 hours more each week than young male professionals.

Such trends to long working hours are exacting a heavy cost on people's personal and family life – costs which came up repeatedly in our focus groups. There is a widespread desire for flexibility that serves the employee rather than just the employer.

Moreover it is not just the obvious groups who want better balance. 51 per cent of young single women and 48 per cent of young single men would like to be able to take a year's unpaid leave (more than any other group); 47 per cent of male single parents would like to be able to work from home;[58] 46 per cent of mothers in relationships would like to be able to take school holidays unpaid; and a quarter of the age group would like their work compressed to 4 days a week. Yet in only very few cases do existing jobs offer any of these options.

The work men want and the work men get

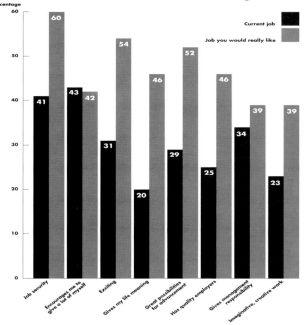

Percentage

Current job
Job you would really like

	Job security	Encourages me to give a lot of myself	Exciting	Gives my life meaning	Great possibilities for advancement	Has quality employers	Gives management responsibility	Imaginative, creative work
Current job	41	43	31	20	29	25	34	23
Job you would really like	60	42	54	46	52	46	39	39

Source: Socioconsult (Base, 18-34 year old men currently in work, 265)

The work women want and the work women get

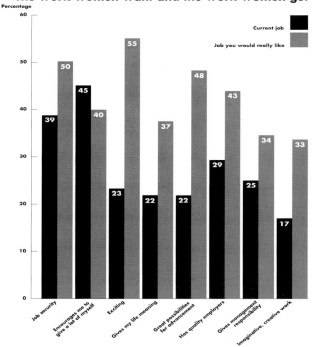

Percentage

Current job
Job you would really like

	Job security	Encourages me to give a lot of myself	Exciting	Gives my life meaning	Great possibilities for advancement	Has quality employers	Gives management responsibility	Imaginative, creative work
Current job	39	45	23	22	22	29	25	17
Job you would really like	50	40	55	37	48	43	34	33

Source: Socioconsult (Base, 18-34 year old women currently in work, 194)

A new deal at work

So although young people's values are in some respects changing in tandem with the world of work the main message is one of confusion and frustration. There is a recognition that the labour market is more fluid, and that more responsibility for skills and careers now falls on the individual.[59] But there is far less clarity about precisely what this means in terms of the core relationship in work: that between employee and employer. The 'old deal' which offered a career or a steady job in an organisation, has disintegrated without anything to replace it. How much is training the responsibility of the firm or individual? Can the employee depend on the firm to provide a pension and other benefits? How much job security can they expect? And if they are female, or a member of an ethnic minority, how much can they expect their employer to care about equal opportunities, rather than seeing this as the responsibility of the state?

Restoring trust

At the heart of the issue is the question of trust. The fracturing of old certainties has left a crisis of confidence right across the labour market. One recent survey of 2,000 middle managers found them to be angry, anxious, distrustful, demotivated and cynical, with declining corporate loyalty.[60] According to the Henley Centre only 15 per cent of the public trust large multinational firms to be honest and, in general, employers are becoming less important as sources of influence, relative to friends, family and work colleagues.[61]

In our focus groups we have been struck by the extent to which young people are instinctively trusting their organisations less and depending on themselves more: many were reconsidering their commitment to their current job or planning escape routes.[62] Others who were about to enter the labour market recognised that whereas their fathers' generation traded boring work for lifelong security, they are being offered boring work without anything in return. But perhaps the best symptom of distrust is to be found in attitudes to pensions, where our survey from *Socioconsult* shows that a remarkable 42 per cent of men aged 25-34 fear that they won't receive the occupational pension they're owed.[63] At the same time nearly two-thirds of 16-24 year old women work for employers who don't even offer any kind of occupational pension.

David Cannon notes that "young people's list of 'What not to trust' has grown very long indeed. You cannot trust your parents to stay together, you cannot trust that your education will lead anywhere and you cannot trust your employers to provide secure jobs for either you or your parents. The economic insecurity familiar only to the working class of the past has now become the everyday reality of the middle class."[64] The result is to see employment in transactional terms, with the priority being 'to keep your options open'.

Some employers may conclude that none of this matters: a low trust environment is either inevitable or even desirable. With a properly competitive market, the role of the employer is simply to buy labour at the lowest possible price. But low trust carries a high cost. In very simple ways it makes it harder to run an organisation (for example confidential information has to be managed far more carefully). Temporary workers don't develop much commitment or the ability to work in a team.[65] Short-term employment contracts can actually reduce flexibility – particularly if labour market conditions tighten.[66] For the individuals themselves the costs are obvious, and often affect their families too. And for the society and economy as a whole low trust tends to result in under-investment in everything from training to physical assets, and (as writers such as Robert Puttnam and Francis Fukuyama have shown) general underperformance.[67]

Rebuilding trust will mean different things in different firms. But there are some general guidelines.

One is simply that openness and honesty – even about unpleasant decisions such as redundancies – tend to pay dividends, not least because they encourage employees to flag up problems before they become crises.

A second is that in many fields it is more efficient to retain some long-term commitments to employees, with task flexibility as the quid pro quo, rather than always seeking maximum job flexibility (Rover is one example).

A third is that it is wise to help those whose employment future is uncertain through training schemes.[68] A fourth is to rethink employee benefits packages to fit changing values:[69] Ford achieved much with its famous EDAP programme for employees to develop non-vocational skills. Another is to help employees to think through their own life goals (as IBM UK did with its 'Fit for the Future' self development course).

But for employees in small firms, or in high turnover occupations, these models are not likely to be on offer. Given that forecasters expect 50 per cent of private sector jobs to be in firms with less than 50 employees by 2000, there is an urgent need for new strategies which offer a degree of security and stability. A role could be played by TECs, for example sponsoring skills and mutual support clubs. Others would benefit from a greater role for what we call 'deployers' – firms which have a long term relationship with individuals and deploy and sell on their labour to others. This model already exists in fields like clerical and secretarial work, in care in the public sector, and increasingly higher up the income scale. Firms like Manpower (already one of the UK's top ten employers, with some 60-65,000 workers on their books) sell people's time to firms but retain a long term relationship with their staff and a commitment to training, pensions and holidays. This 'agency' model could conceivably provide a more reliable core relationship in the workplace and could be encouraged through tax policies which reverse the current disincentives against employer commitment.

Training: whose responsibility?

For many the key symbol of trust is training. Today's young people know that their future depends on skills – preferably transferable ones. We found that many who left school without qualifications now regret it.[70] But who will provide them with the skills? Our analysis of the BHPS found that 65 per cent of 25-34 year olds (in work and out of work), and two-thirds of working women under 35, had not had any training or education in the last 12 months.[71] Yet at the same time employers complain about the lack of vocational skills. Given the need for constant upskilling, and given that nearly 2 in 3 British workers report that the level of skills required for their job has increased in the last five years something is clearly wrong.[72]

For the core workers the business responsibility for training remains, and will be, perhaps even more than in the past, an important symbol of commitment. There is a strong case for policies to encourage or require employers to invest more in skills. However, from a business point of view there is little reason to invest in short-term workers whose skills are easily replaceable either by other workers or by machines.[73] Although employers train a quarter of their graduate employees each month they train only 4 per cent of their staff who have no qualifications.

The general picture for all young employees is that as firms retrench and governments remain fiscally constrained, they will have to take more responsibility for their own skills, including being prepared to pay for courses and qualifications themselves. Many will have to be realistic about the skills they need; as John Tate of BTEC put it 'parents' prejudices [against vocational skills] which they pass on to young people are the biggest challenge we face'.[74]

No one has yet gone to their bank manager to ask for a mortgage for an NVQ rather than a house. But in the future this could become commonplace, and, for this generation, there is a strong case for weighting any tax incentives far more to human capital than to physical capital or housing.

From equality to diversity

The third unresolved area is equal opportunities. During the 1980s equal opportunities policies moved from the politically-motivated public sector into business. Many companies have introduced targets and family friendly policies, encouraged by organisations like Opportunity 2000, and persuaded by the business case that giving women and ethnic minorities better chances to develop their potential is good for competitiveness. The result has been a climate in which young women managers and professionals have made important advances and in which the culture of many large firms is shifting towards greater openness and equality.

However, equality of opportunity has not been achieved, and certainly has not filtered down to low-paid jobs. The limit of the business case is that there is often little incentive to invest in the opportunities of less skilled women workers, or to address the widening pay gap between women, rather than between women and men. Moreover many policies still seem peripheral, and are rarely integrated into broader career development strategies, or indeed policies for time.

Targets, which have been set in many organisations, have become the main focus for a far-reaching rethink of equal opportunities. This rethink has mirrored the debate in the US where affirmative action initiatives were from the outset controversial. Many beneficiaries feared that they would be stigmatised as inadequate and that any special treatment would set off a backlash. These fears have been borne out. Preferential selection results in more stress for the individual involved than selection on merit, and many beneficiaries come to feel inadequate, with a 'stigma of incompetence'. According to one report "affirmative action policies can thwart rather than promote workplace equality. The stigma associated with affirmative action can fuel rather than debunk stereotypical thinking and prejudiced attitudes."[75] Moreover the focus on groups by definition ignores differences within specific groups – for example the needs of educated professional women relative to unskilled female workers, or school-leaver blacks relative to those with university education.

But the core lesson from the US is that affirmative action, ironically, seems to clash with what may be the most central value of society: the idea that everybody should be treated equally. Special treatment for any group seems to clash with this principle, whether it takes the form of quotas (as in the USA) or targets (which are the main tool in Britain since quotas are illegal).

The starkest weakness of these types of policy is that they are ineffective. A recent survey of 285 companies' career development initiatives found that targets and positive action initiatives in recruitment advertising were the least successful tools.[76] By contrast, the two most successful were introducing equal rights and benefits for part-time workers relative to full-time workers and allowing flexibility in uniform/dress requirements. In other words the least successful initiatives were those with a specific group focus whilst the most successful ones tackled inequality laterally. The authors of the study, Rajvinder Kandola and Johanna Fullerton, argue that "if actions are to be addressed to particular groups a hierarchy will develop of those groups that will get priority attention at any particular time. This may lead to frustration and even resentment on the part of those who feel excluded. It also highlights the point that equal opportunities is seen as being about and for women, ethnic minorities and people with disabilities. Nobody mentioned as a priority area getting men into non-traditional areas of work!"

It may have been inevitable that mistakes would be made in the first wave of equal opportunities policies. Certainly, many organisations seem to have set unrealistic targets, whether in relation to the supply of labour or internal opportunities. Others have time limited their targets, and then forced change through too fast, exacerbating resentment.[77]

In some cases targets have been well-designed and effective. But in most cases they seem to be unpopular with women as well as men[78] – not just because of fears of male hostility, but also because of fears of the self-doubt that arises from not believing you are the right person for a job. The result is a reluctance to support schemes targeted solely at women.[79] Most want to be treated 'as an individual and a person first, not as a number or as a woman'.

The next phase of equal opportunities is already moving away from the crude tools of the past.[80] The keys now are diversity strategies within which careers can be helped for all groups of employees; special measures which target groups (such as part-timers) within which women and ethnic minorities are over represented; and workforce projections as opposed to targets which set a frame for managers.

But these will only touch part of the workforce. Business cannot realistically be expected to do much for the opportunities of workers without scarce skills. With the shift to smaller firms and more contingent relationships the whole paraphernalia of equal opportunities will need to be rethought (including the roles of the Equal Opportunities Commission and Commission for Racial Equality) with ever more attention to 'upstream' causes (such as skills) rather than 'downstream' effects.

Fitting work to parenting

Despite the partial progress in equal opportunities, few jobs are family friendly. Our analysis of the BHPS finds that 98 per cent of 25-34 year old women believe employers should help with childcare, but few do. In practice, instead of relying on employers to help, younger women are more likely to depend on their partner than older generations and nearly twice as likely to use formal child care (a nanny, nursery or childminder). They are also more likely to depend on a relative, friend or neighbour, and differ from older mothers in being much less likely to shape their work around the children's needs by, for example, only working when children are at school.

Childcare arrangements for women (%)

Age	Work*	Spouse	Formal	Kin
16-34	25.4	26.8	23.1	24.8
35-55	49.4	19.7	12.0	18.9

Source: British Household Panel Study (Base, all working women with children, 614)

* Work is fitted around children's needs and school hours

As the table below shows there are important class differences. 77.4 per cent of professional women depend on formal child care, compared to only 35.8 per cent of managerial and technical workers and 27.3 per cent of skilled non manual workers. By contrast unskilled workers depend mainly on their spouse, as do a quarter of women in managerial and technical jobs.[81]

Childcare arrangements by social class, 16-34 year old women (%)

Job description	Childcare provider			
	Work*	Spouse	Formal	Family
Professional occupation	22.6	0.0	77.4	0.0
Managerial and technical	15.4	25.1	35.8	23.7
Skilled non-manual	24.3	22.3	27.3	26.2
Skilled manual	22.6	21.9	18.4	37.1
Partly skilled	38.6	33.6	8.0	19.8
Unskilled	27.7	44.6	0.0	27.7

Source: British Household Panel Survey (Base, all working women aged 16-34 with children, 311)

*Work is fitted around children's needs and school hours

We have already seen how the costs of having a child have grown for many women. What could be done to make these trade-offs more bearable? Clearly for employers there is a good case for being family friendly, particularly with scarcer staff, and there is now a range of best practice to draw from, including term-time working and parental leave. These seem to offer tangible benefits. A survey conducted in America found that workplace policies which accommodate the family needs of employees are likely to lead to improvements in job satisfaction, reduced absenteeism rates, and greater willingness to do unpaid overtime and to work later into pregnancy. It also found that 78 per cent of female employees were likely to return to work after childbirth in firms with family friendly policies compared to only 52 per cent in unaccommodating workplaces.[82] Family friendly practice can also help in improving attitudes towards work and behaviour at work.[83] Similar results have been reported in the UK: one survey found that 50 per cent of managers reported that their work performance had improved after working flexibly and 64 per cent that their quality of life had improved.[84]

But too often such family friendly initiatives are seen as add-ons; they don't impact on the dominant work culture (with its stress on very long hours), or on career development policies. Moreover because they don't usually address the desire for time off of other groups – such as single men – they fail to build sufficiently broad support.[85] In our view companies need to move from the model of family friendliness to a broader work/life model which avoids the problems of group specificity but which nevertheless benefits those groups most in need.[86]

But firms on their own cannot be expected to carry the costs of making work more life and family friendly. If as a society we wish women to be able to have children, without giving up their chances in jobs and careers, policies will have to change. As we argue in the next chapter, what is needed is not just a raft of measures to reduce the economic costs of having a child (for example through subsidising parental leave) but also measures to help women who leave the labour market to get back, with targeted training packages for parents.

Other countries and companies outside the UK have certainly done much more. Scandinavian countries and Australia have been particularly impressive. Significantly, in a recent European Union competition for family friendly companies, not one British company made the top ten.[87]

The non-linear career

If we accept a much less structured work environment as a given, how can individuals cope with autonomy? An important step is to rethink the career. Most firms are still attached to the old idea of a hierarchical, linear career. As Professor Cary Cooper and Dr Suzan Lewis[88] argue this model fails to take into account the prevalence of increasing burnout, midlife crises, career changes and the redundancies (and sideways and downwards shifts) of employees in their fifties. Moreover, too often the transition to 'flatter structures' looks like an excuse for too little care for the employee, rather than enriching careers.

Any credible career strategies have to prepare people for more varied working patterns; for using time out of work constructively; and for accumulating generic skills rather than the more specific ones that employers will tend to prefer. For the employer this may simply require a commitment to time release schemes to enable individuals to train themselves; but larger ones will need to develop career targets (preferably devised for the individual), strategies for meeting them if they are to be credible, and benchmarks against which progress can be measured. In general there is a need for more complex, lateral and non-linear career paths which make it easier for people to take sabbaticals and to move out of more senior roles without this entailing a loss of status and recognition.

Choice over time

We have argued elsewhere[89] for a new balance of responsibility between the individual, the employer and the state to cope with, and pay for, more varied uses of time. This might involve such things as lifetime rights to tertiary education combined with income-contingent repayment schemes, secured on lifetime earnings and repaid through the Inland Revenue, rights to unpaid educational leave,[90] and rights to parental leave (and rights to reclaiming jobs up to five years). Much the same rights to retain a job and to time off will be needed for making it easier to look after elderly or sick relatives.

The best symbol of a new attitude to time is the sabbatical. In more pressurised and longer lives, we need breaks all the more: opportunities to try out tasks, to learn new skills or even just to have fun. At the moment sabbaticals are an elite luxury. They have no legal backing in the UK and few dare ask for them in insecure jobs markets. Some firms offer them to older employees (John Lewis for example gives 6 months paid leave after 25 years work) but these are a reward for service not something integrated into the rhythms of life. In order to make these more widely available the law needs to provide support. France and Belgium already offer legal rights – 6-12 months in Belgium, 11 in France.

The priority in the future will be to develop more flexible funding schemes. Singapore's Central Provident Fund is one example, which now provides funding not only for retirement and medical care but also for further education, based on compulsory contributions from employees and employers which are paid regardless of whether employees are part-time or temporary. But the likelihood is that we will need more complicated hybrids, combining personal funding, government support and employer obligations.

Casualties of change

People in work – at all ages – are strikingly happier than those out of work. In every age group working women, even if they have children, are happier than women who are at home.

For these reasons alone we should be extremely

concerned about the high levels of unemployment in this age group. The vast majority of unemployed young men are keen to work[91] and our BHPS analysis shows that most women under 35 who are not in work would like a regular paid job even if only for a few hours a week. For many single parents, too, work is a vital link to the wider society.

Yet in practice a large group is becoming steadily disconnected from work. 15 per cent of adults now live in households with no earners.[92] Many of the unemployed are cynical not only about the jobs on offer to them, but also about the various training schemes on offer.[93] And recent research concludes that 'more of the non-employed population are losing attachment to the labour market.'[94] What can be done? In our view the priority is to bring two main groups back into work:

Unemployed young men
Men have borne the brunt of changes at work. For them work was the main source of identity and the means by which they defined their manhood. Now, for a minority, crime has filled the vacuum as an alternative lifestyle, while for others the loss of identity is simply debilitating.[95] Although the numbers entering the jobs market are likely to fall, the problem is likely to get worse. As the Institute of Fiscal Studies has shown, unskilled teenage men now entering the jobs market will probably see their incomes decline still further.[96] The costs of men's declining status are already clear, particularly for young black men: a dramatic increase in male suicide, a rise in male depression and signs that many young men are trapped in a form of 'permanent adolescence', unable to make the transition into adulthood.

New policy problems are fast coming onto the agenda. One is male underachievement in schools. Another is discrimination. Many young unskilled men feel that they are excluded from 'women's jobs', and many employers feel they have an interest in selecting women who demand less wages. In this respect the recent EOC ruling which found a firm guilty of reserving jobs for women was an important landmark given that 20 years after the passing of equal opportunities legislation the EOC now receives more complaints from men than from women about job advertisements and employers' preferences. Just as we need to think vigorously about breaking down the barriers to jobs for women, we also need to break down the barriers of discrimination and culture that prevent young men from getting many jobs in services.

However such policies will only marginally meet the needs of the current generation of young men. Some policies will probably help – such as providing a proper one-stop advisory service, and subsidising employers to give trials to, and take on, unemployed young people. But government will probably also need again to take on its historic role (dating back to ancient Rome) as an employer of last resort.

What might this mean? As Demos has argued elsewhere schemes of job creation, or paid community service, are no easy panacea for today's young people. They need to tap people's self interest, rather than altruism, by giving tangible benefits – money, skills, or some other benefit such as the chance to build or renovate a home. We have produced detailed proposals for an alternative CONNECT scheme,[97] as well as suggesting how benefits could be adapted to encourage the unemployed to become involved in useful activities which are not necessarily paid jobs. We are also developing models whereby young people could join clubs which would combine work with other benefits, rather as the successful foyer schemes combine work, housing and personal development.[98] Most of these entail substantial costs (the idea that getting people into work saves government money is largely an illusion), and no government will lightly commit to providing a job to all unemployed young people. But the alternative is likely to be a further disconnection from society and its values.

Schemes of this kind will suffer if they seem to be targetted at young people as a 'problem group'. That is why there is a case for linking community service and job creation for young people to Community Service for Older People. There are precedents. Both France and Germany introduced schemes to encourage early retirement in the early 1980s[99] and in Britain the Job Release Scheme introduced in 1977 alleviated unemployment amongst young people by providing allowances for older people to take earlier retirement. At its peak in 1984/85 some 90,000 older people were receiving allowances.[100] In Americans the partial system of national service for seniors which has developed over 30 years[101] is being built up, not only so as to draw on old people's energies but also to create a bridge between the generations. Linking old and young in common schemes, and providing parallel support to employ young and old people part-time to ease transitions in and out of the labour market, would help remove the stigma that many young people resent.

Policies of this kind are difficult to get precisely right. But they meet a public mood. We found strong support for progressive reductions in the working hours of over 55s so as to offer jobs to the young, and 45 per cent of 18-34 year olds see it as either inevitable or desirable that they should take a 10 per cent cut in salary to avoid job losses or create new ones. Translating those attitudes into behaviour is hard, and depends on schemes being credible. But there is no reason why this should be impossible.

Single parents
The vast majority of single parents are women – and particularly numerous in this generation. Our analysis of the *Socioconsult* survey finds that on almost every key indicator single parents are one of the most disconnected groups. They are more likely to live in poverty than families with two parents, less likely to be

in work and are all too often stigmatised in policy debates as burdens on the state. Moreover because of the structure of the tax/benefits system many find that in the absence of affordable and high quality child care, they are better off financially if they do not work.

Many argue that single parents should be encouraged back to work to save money. Australia's Jobs, Education and Training Programme specifically targets lone parents and has over the last five years reached nearly half of that group, significantly raising levels of training, employment and earnings. Its claimed savings have consistently outstripped targets and are now close to the overall programme costs Crucial to JET's success is the link to effective child care: lone parents in training or jobs receive priority in publicly funded child care services, and the JET programme can finance a temporary extra child care place.[102]

Certainly there are aspects of the JET scheme which could be introduced into Britain. But it would be naive to think that the scheme will be cost effective for all lone parents. Many are unskilled and relatively uneducated and will be working in low paid jobs – the costs of child care may not be much less than what they can earn. It would be wrong to justify such schemes primarily in economic terms. Instead their major virtue is more likely to be a social one – reconnecting the many single parents who feel cut off from the rest of society. This is also why there is a case for linking them to the kinds of community service described in the Demos CONNECT scheme, which would enable single parents to club together to work part-time while also providing shared childcare and other services without losing benefits.

Conclusion
Each of these policy areas – from training and family-friendly schemes, to work creation – is really about one thing: using work to re-establish the connections across society and between the generations, connections that

have become frayed over the last few decades.

Many people have benefitted enormously from the changes in work in recent decades. Their opportunities to shape their careers and control their own destinies are far greater than those of previous generations. This is why it would be wrong to reverse the shift to a more individualised model of work. But taken too far this model leaves people too vulnerable and too isolated. That is why we need to find a better balance between flexibility and commitment for employees at all levels so that work can contribute to life rather than constrain it.

Renegotiating relationships and parenting

Recent decades have brought an extraordinary liberation in personal relationships. The constraints that kept millions of women and men in unhappy marriages and that stopped them from taking control of their own sexuality and commitments, have largely disappeared.

But nowhere has freedom caused more disorientation than in family life, and it is common now to see family life portrayed as a war zone, full of conflict and collateral damage,mainly for children.

But what should be done? Can the strands linking marriage, parenting and sex be remade? Should we seek to revive the nuclear family, Victorian values or even orphanages as some have argued? Do we have to forgo newly won freedoms in order to have good relationships and supportive structures for children?

In this chapter we explain the major changes affecting the 18-34 generation, before setting out the far-reaching changes which we believe will be necessary to provide a sustainable balance between commitments and freedom.

The new landscape of relationships
The retreat from marriage

The retreat from marriage has been the most visible indicator of change. Its popularity is at a 50 year low whilst the divorce rate is at an all time high.[1] An institution that was once an unquestioned part of the fabric of life has now become a matter of personal choice. Partly this is a matter of people exiting marriage. Following a sixfold rise in the divorce rate between 1961 and 1991,[2] Britain now has the highest rate of divorces in Europe[3] with four out of ten marriages predicted to end in divorce.[4]

But it is also a matter of people rejecting marriage in the first place. Whereas 95 per cent of women born in Western Europe in 1950 will marry at some point in their lifetime only 78 per cent of women born in 1960 are expected to do so.[5] If the golden age of marriage was between 1950 and 1970, when post war prosperity helped to produce a marriage boom,[6] since the early 1970s the marriage rate has halved, and today, each year, more than a third of all marriages are remarriages.[7]

Marriage is certainly losing its appeal for this generation. First time marriages are now at their lowest level since 1889[8] and amongst those born in 1961 62 per cent of men and 74 per cent of women were married by the age of 30 compared to 78 per cent of men and 88 per cent of women born in 1951.[9] A sign of this more contingent attitude is the extent to which people are postponing their big day. In 1971 men married for the first time at an average age of 22 whilst today the average age is 27. In 1971 the average age of first time brides was 20; by 1992 it was 26.[10]

There are both small and big reasons for this. One of the smaller ones is the price of marriage. The average white wedding costs around £8,500,[11] and in one study 22 per cent of long term cohabiting mothers cited cost as an important reason for not getting married.[12] Certainly the marriage 'boom' of the 1950s and 1960s was helped by general prosperity (and the ease with which people could move away from their parents into the marital home),[13] just as the biggest falls in marriage in the early 1990s were in those regions most affected by the recession.[14]

But the main reasons for declining confidence in marriage are more fundamental. Marriage is no longer a reliable institution. One tenth of women who married in 1951 were divorced by their Silver Wedding anniversary; the same proportion marrying a decade later had divorced by their fifteenth year of marriage whilst a tenth of women marrying in 1987 had divorced by the end of their fourth year of marriage.[15] Not surprisingly trends of this kind make people more wary – one study found that 30 per cent of unmarried mothers cite the fear of divorce as a disincentive to marriage.[16]

Behind these trends lies freedom: the combination of economic independence and women's rising aspiration for autonomy – in particular their own personal and social development. In our qualitative research many women said that their own personal development had accelerated relationship breakdown, and some 72 per cent of all divorces are now initiated by women[17]. Research has also shown that right across the world women's financial need for marriage declines as their pay rises relative to men.[18] Given the continuing momentum towards equalising pay, there are good reasons for expecting the divorce rate to get worse before it gets better.

But values are also changing how marriage is seen. Whereas in 1955 couples stressed the efficient fulfilment of the roles of breadwinner and homemaker as the most important thing in marriage, by 1970 both men and women said that the key was for men and women to love each other.[19] The 1986 British Social Attitudes study too found that faithfulness, mutual respect, understanding and tolerance, were the most frequently cited qualities whilst good housing, shared religious and political beliefs and similar social backgrounds had become less important.[20] Our qualitative research has also confirmed that couples now place much more weight on emotional intimacy, mutual affection, and sexual fulfilment.

This shift from 'marriage as an institution' to 'marriage as a relationship'[21] has many implications. It renders it a more personal and private fact, less tied into kinship; it renders it less an economic and more an emotional relationship; and it places it within a large culture of choice.

The problem, however, is that this shift inevitably fuels high expectations. As one author puts it: "Couples today have greater expectations of their partners not only as spouses but as individuals, and there is a greater possibility of disappointment. Meeting these new expectations brings fresh challenges for which there are no traditions to draw on nor known roles to emulate."[22]

More contingent attitudes also encourage greater unfaithfulness. 83 per cent of the population think that 'extra marital affairs are always or almost always wrong', but in fact we are probably more adulterous now than ever before and women are catching up with men on the adultery stakes.

Before 1960, while the typical unfaithful bride waited 14 years before taking a lover, their husbands strayed after eight years. In contrast brides marrying after 1970 waited just four years whilst their husbands waited five years.[23]

All in all, whether the cause is longevity,[24] secularisation,[25] or simply a culture of freedom the effect has been to remove much of the stigma both of adultery and of marital breakdown for a younger generation. Carol Smart, a sociologist from Leeds University, argues that a new kind of marriage is emerging, one in which people 'enter relationships for specific benefits and leave marriages if these benefits are not delivered.'[26] The marriage contract, like the employment contract, is increasingly seen in these transactional terms.

The rise of cohabitation

The return of widespread cohabitation (which involved up to a fifth of couples before the mid-nineteenth century), has become the clearest sign of the rise of contingent relationships, with no legal ties, and mutual obligations which can be revoked at any time. The trends are clear cut. There has been a fourfold increase in the numbers of people cohabiting before marriage over the last four decades,[27] and nearly half of women born in the 1960s have cohabited compared with only 19 per cent born in the 1940s and 4 per cent born in the 1920s.[28] Thus whereas a young woman in the 1960s typically began her first sexual relationship at marriage around the age of 23, a decade later women were becoming sexually active in their late teens but marrying later at 24.[29]

A generation ago the middle classes pioneered cohabitation. But amongst a younger generation the class difference has all but disappeared and, as the graphs opposite show, whereas marriage was still the dominant way of entering a partnership for women born between 1950-1962, cohabitation rather than marriage is the dominant way of entering a partnership for women under 32.[30] By 2000 it is forecast that four out of five married couples will have lived together before marriage.[31]

While cohabitation still remains a prelude to marriage for the majority, there are now signs of more permanent cohabitation patterns amongst a younger generation. Whereas 65 per cent of women born between 1950-62 who were cohabiting went on to marry, this is expected to be true of only 56 per cent of those born after 1962.[32] Not surprisingly, these behavioural shifts are both the cause and effect of changing values. The crucial generational difference, and the starkest point of tension, is the extent to which younger generations have thrown off the moral taboo about living together. Fewer than one in ten young people feel that living together outside marriage is wrong compared with more than one in three in the oldest age cohort[33] and less than 7 per cent of women born after 1960 agree that 'living together before marriage is always wrong' compared to 35 per cent of women born before 1930.[34]

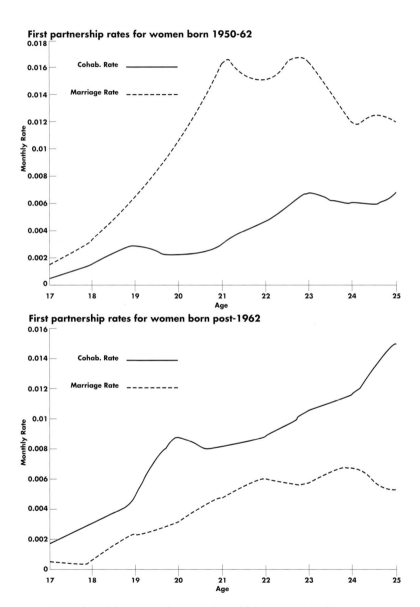

First partnership rates for women born 1950-62

Cohab. Rate ————

Marriage Rate - - - - - - -

First partnership rates for women born post-1962

Cohab. Rate ————

Marriage Rate - - - - - - -

Source: John Ermisch, ESRC Research Centre on Micro-Social Change, Essex University

A significant minority, 21 per cent, are simply against marriage as an institution.[35] For most young people, however, living together is simply the 'sensible' option,[36] a form of 'trial marriage'.[37] The British Social Attitudes survey for 1989 found that 59 per cent of 18-24 year olds would recommend that people should cohabit before marriage compared to just 25 per cent of 55-59 year olds.[38]

Cohabitation may prepare people better for marriage. It should mean fewer battles over who does the washing up, and fewer tensions over personal habits. But it has its own problems. Its lack of commitment means that cohabiting couples' sexual behaviour is more similar to people who are single, divorced, or separated than to married couples.[39] One study found that 23 per cent saw cohabitation as a viable alternative to marriage precisely because it gives the individuals concerned greater freedom and autonomy without legal ties. [40] Perhaps because of this, cohabiting couples are four times more likely than married couples to split up.[41] Once again there is a clear generational trend. Two-fifths of cohabiting relationships involving women under 32 are expected to dissolve within 10 years.[42] Perhaps most telling is the fact that although many people cohabit as a way of 'testing the waters' before actually committing to marriage itself, married couples are actually more, not less, likely to divorce if they have lived together first.[43]

Parenting pains
Parenting is also becoming less of a given. Firstly, fewer children are being born. The average number of children per woman declined rapidly in the late 1960s and 1970s, and has now levelled off at about 1.8, below the replacement level of 2.1.[44] Secondly, women are having children later (the average age for a first child is now 28.1, up from 23.6 in 1971[45]) and there has been a 33 per cent increase in the number of women having children in their forties in the past decade.[46] In 1992, for the first

time, more children were being born to women in their early thirties than women in their early twenties.[47] These trends are set to continue: according to MORI *Socioconsult* 29 per cent of women aged between 18-34, and 51 per cent of men, want 'to delay having children as long as possible'. Some women are opting out of motherhood altogether.[48] The number of women aged between 16-49 who say that they expect to remain childless has doubled between 1986 and 1991 and there is a clear generational effect. The younger you are the more likely you are to want to remain childless, and more than 20 per cent of women born in 1967 are predicted to be childless at 40 compared with 13 per cent of those born in 1947.[49] Others have forecast that a fifth of women born in the 60s, 70s and 80s will remain childless for all of their lives.[50]

Meanwhile for those who do have children, the traditional links between marriage and parenthood have gone. About one third of babies are now born outside of wedlock (up from just 6 per cent in 1961[51]), and whereas only 9 per cent of women born between 1950 and 1962 gave birth to a child whilst cohabiting this is expected to double to 18 per cent for women born after 1962.[52] Perhaps not surprisingly less than half of under 25 year olds surveyed in 1989 thought that people who want children ought to get married whereas 90 per cent of those under 55 thought they should.[53]

What does this mean for children? As many as one in four children in England and Wales will see their parents' divorce before they are 16,[54] and amongst unmarried women born after 1962, two-fifths of one parent families result from a cohabiting relationship that has broken down.[55] Every year 3 per cent of children experience parental separation and 2.5 per cent experience either the arrival of a step-parent or the return of a natural parent[56] (and the National Step Family Association predicts that by 2000 2.5 million children will be growing up with one or more step-parents).[57]

But although children have often lost out from more flexible relationships there has also been one other, potentially crucial change in the perception of parenting. Children's status is increasingly recognised, both in law through the Children's Act and in our culture. They are no longer simply there to be seen but not heard. Instead our figures from *Socioconsult* show that 87.3 per cent of women and 76 per cent of men aged between 18-34 agree that 'children should have the right to participate in family decision making'.

Single parents
One of the most controversial effects of changing relationships has been the steady rise in the numbers of lone parents. There are now around 1.4m, of whom 90 per cent are women[58], and, in 1992, divorcees were for the first time in 1992 outnumbered by parents who had never been married.[59] Our analysis of the BHPS finds that the proportion of lone mothers is now 13.3 per cent amongst 25-34 year olds, the highest of any age group, although the ratio of single mothers to couples with children is actually higher (55 per cent) amongst 16-24 year olds.

Despite the stigmatisation of lone parents younger people seem to take them for granted.[60] 75.4 per cent of 16-24 year old women and 72 per cent of 25-34 year olds think that single parents can bring up children as well as a couple compared to only 41.2 per cent of women over 55. There is a similar pattern for men.

Response to statement 'A single parent can bring up children as well as a couple' (%)

		Age			
		16-24	25-34	35-55	56yrs+
Agree	Women	75.4	72.2	59.2	41.2
	Men	52.9	47.2	33.9	20.9
Disagree	Women	24.6	27.8	40.8	58.8
	Men	47.1	52.8	66.1	79.1

Source: British Household Panel Study (Base, 6816)

But single parents are not at ease with their place in society, not least because of their stigmatisation by people in power. As we shall see, they are in many ways the most disconnected group. Many are also hostile to men and any claims they might have to be more involved in parenting: whereas 90 per cent of women in all age groups agree that fathers should be involved in bringing up children, our analysis of the BHPS shows that this falls to 63 per cent for 25-34 year old single mothers.

Household equality

The fifth trend is towards greater equality in the home, and an unravelling of the old gender division of labour. Whilst almost 63 per cent of women aged over 55 agree that 'a husband should earn and the wife should stay at home', this falls sharply to 18 per cent amongst 35-55 year olds and just 8.4 per cent amongst 16-24 year old women. There is a similar pattern with men.

There are good economic reasons for this. Given that over the last twenty years alone women's contribution to family income has risen from one quarter to one third,[61] it no longer makes such sense for women to forgo earnings. In our qualitative research we found that even young men holding more 'traditional' values are having to adapt their attitudes to fit with economic necessity. Whatever the causes, the shift to greater equality can be seen on several different dimensions.

A first is household management. Our analysis shows that the housekeeping allowance is now an anachronism to a younger generation, regardless of whether the woman is working or not. Just 4 per cent of non-working women aged between 16-24 now get a housekeeping allowance while their partner looks after the rest of the money, compared to 21 per cent aged 35-55. At the same time younger women are also becoming less willing to bear the burden of managing household finances. Only 22 per cent of working women aged between 16-24 say that they look after the household finances compared to

29 per cent of 35-55 year olds. The shift to shared management continues with 62 per cent of 16-24 year old working women agreeing that they share and manage the household finances jointly compared to 52 per cent of 35-55 year old working women.

A second indicator is household labour. Our *Socioconsult* survey shows that 92 per cent of 18-34 year old women and 89 per cent of men believe that couples should take equal responsibility for household chores. In fact, working women aged between 18-34 still do more even than non-working men of the same age. But as the table below shows this imbalance masks a profound change: the ratio of the time spent by working women relative to men in cooking, cleaning and doing the laundry has fallen from 3 amongst 35-55 year olds to 2.3 for 25-34 year olds and just 1.75 for 16-24 year olds. Perhaps even more striking is the fact that the amount of time spent by the youngest working women is barely a third of the time spent by the oldest working women.

Hours spent doing domestic work in a week

	Age		
	16-24	25-34	35-55
Working Women	7	14	18
Working Men	4	6	6

Source: British Household Panel Study (Base, 4348)

At this rate of change we might expect the gender gap to have disappeared within a decade or so. Perhaps too, despite hi-tech washing machines and hoovers, the young are becoming the dirty generation as masculinised new women accept male standards of cleanliness rather than the other way around.[62] Much the same story can be found from our analysis of the BHPS data for other household tasks such as cooking (16.7 per cent of 35-55 year old women share cooking compared to 34.1 per cent of 16-24 year olds), and cleaning (18.9 per cent of 35-55 year old women share cleaning compared to 25.5 per cent of 16-24 year old women).[63]

Third, we also find a greater flexibility in attitudes to parenting. In our analysis of the BHPS we found strong support for the idea that the father should play a full role in parenting – 92 per cent of 16-34 years agree with this. At the same time, and as the table below shows, younger people are significantly less likely to agree that 'family life suffers if the mother works full-time' (22.3 per cent of women aged 16-24 compared to 69.4 per cent of women aged over 55). There is a similar trend for men: 29.9 per cent of 16-24 year olds agree compared to 80.1 per cent of men over 55.

Response to statement 'Family life suffers if mother works full-time' (%)

		Age			
		16-24	25-34	35-55	56yrs+
Agree	Women	22.3	36.3	49.2	69.4
	Men	29.9	37.1	54.7	80.1
Disagree	Women	77.7	63.7	50.8	30.6
	Men	70.1	62.9	45.3	19.9

Source: British Household Panel Study (Base, 6510)

One result of this equalisation is that younger parents are more likely to depend on a husband or partner and less likely to shape their work around their family's needs.

Finally, there is friendship. We find that 87 per cent of women and 82.6 per cent of men aged between 18-34 agree that 'both partners should have their own circle of friends'.[64]

It would be wrong to exaggerate these trends. Men themselves acknowledge that most young women – 69.3 per cent of 25-34 year olds – still take primary responsibility for child care (compared to only 2.8 per cent of men) and our figures from the BHPS show that 65 per cent of women look after children if they are ill compared to just 11 per cent of their spouses. More interestingly two-thirds of working mothers under 35 pay for their own child care (on average, £35 each week, although some women are paying as much as £200 each week); only 28 per cent share the costs with their partner and only in 6 per cent of households do partners bear the cost. In other words, there is still a fiscal gender division of labour with women paying for child care as the price for going out to work.

The rise of gay households
There have always been gay couples and gay households. But only in the last 20-30 years have gays become a more normal part of British society, particularly in cities like London and Manchester which have far higher proportions of gays than other areas. Attitudes are changing steadily. 16-24 year old men are more likely to report having been attracted to someone of the same gender.[65] For this age group 'coming out' no longer has the same frightening significance that it once did. Amongst the public the proportion seeing homosexuality as wrong has fallen from 74 per cent in 1987 to 64 per cent in 1993. – with younger generations tending to be more tolerant.[66] Despite fears that AIDS would fuel an anti-gay backlash this hasn't happened, and instead the debate is moving forward to achieving equality around the age of consent and gay marriage.[67]

The shrinking household
British households are also shrinking. The average size has fallen from nearly four in 1900, to 2.72 in 1981 and only 2.48 in 1991.[68] This reflects the weakening both of the nuclear family and of the extended family. In the mid-18th century 45 per cent of people over 65 lived with a child, whereas fewer than 10 per cent do today.

The effect has been to change the social geography of Britain, and today more than one quarter of all households in Great Britain have only one occupant, almost double the proportion in 1961,[69] and a likely cause of profound pressure on housing markets in the years ahead (since the implication is that we will need 4 million new homes by 2010).

There are many reasons for this. One is simply longevity. There has been a dramatic rise in the number of elderly people aged over 75 and the numbers over 85 have doubled since 1981.[70] However ageing alone does not explain the acceleration of this trend. It is also a direct effect of the desire for greater autonomy, and of family and relationship breakdown – with one of the main areas of growth being young and middle aged men. For them the single household may be becoming a more attractive base from which to participate in relationships or even parenting. This 'intimacy at a distance was highlighted in a recent report by the Department of Environment which predicts that by 2011 there will be 3.1 million bachelors and spinsters in England alone, three times the number in 1971.[72]

Remaking commitment

What do all of these trends add up to? It is worth remembering that the majority of this generation is still getting married, still having children, and still (just about) managing to maintain long-term relationships. But the context is one in which even those institutions which look superficially unchanged are now being used in significantly different ways. So even if a household apparently includes two married parents and two children, the mother is far more likely to work, and far more family decisions are likely to be negotiated rather than imposed by a patriarchal father.

This greater openness, choice and honesty represents great progress. People have been liberated from tradition and social constraints and enabled to seek personal fulfilment and happiness, to choose their own lifestyle and control the terms on which they make relationships. In our qualitative research we found that young people value the greater equality, mutual respect and intimacy that recent years have brought, and in our focus groups we found a strong, optimistic consensus amongst 18-34 year olds that the world of relationships and families has improved greatly compared to their parents' generation.

But it would be unwise to see these freedoms as involving no costs and no new problems. Clearly they do. And it is to these that we now turn.

Relationship breakdown

The most visible side effect of greater freedom has been the rising number of broken relationships. Many find it hard to balance the needs of their families and their own personal desires,[73] and although all relationships depend on compromise and negotiation to survive difficult periods,[74] it seems that this generation lacks either the skills, and perhaps even the will. In our discussion groups many said that their parents' generation tried harder to make their relationships work.

For public policy makers, the heart of the problem is that relationship breakdown is so destructive. We know that the quality of people's relationships is the biggest single source of happiness other than the absence of serious illness,[75] and there is overwhelming evidence of the cost of divorce, which comes second only to the death of a spouse in causing stress.[76] Divorcees tend to be less healthy mentally and physically,[77] and are four times more likely to commit suicide than married people.[78] For many women divorce and separation are also fairly certain routes into poverty.

Children often suffer even more. Children whose parents separate are more likely to experience educational, health and behaviour deficits, more likely to be brought up in poverty, and more likely to divorce themselves when they become adults.[79]

The costs are also felt more widely.[80] Companies bear a burden – estimated at £200 million each year through absenteeism and impaired work efficiency. One estimate put the cost for government of divorce and separation at £3.4 billion each year,[81] and rising numbers of lone parents contribute to spiralling social security costs.[82]

The core problem for public policy, however, is that so

80

much of it is currently directed to picking up the pieces, not to prevention. In the long-run, for the 18-34 generation and those coming after them, the priority must be to help people manage their relationships better, so as to stop the inter-generational transfer of instability in personal relationships. How might this be done?

We need a new set of skills – negotiating skills, ways of making deals and compromises, conflict resolution skills[83] – the kinds of skills that owe more to a boardroom or war-time negotiation table than to romance. These have to be learnt and taught. Schools (and extracurricular activities) need to be better designed to help people develop inter-personal skills for friendships and relationships.

Unfortunately such policies do not address the needs of the current generation. Some voluntary agencies such as RELATE are already doing preventative work through their Training and Education Service. They are actively involved in marriage preparation, as well as working with separated and divorced parents and step parents.[84] They have also recently set up an arm for adolescents called RELATEEN, in recognition of the fact that younger generations are finding it hard to sustain long term relationships.

But most people won't seek this kind of help. One survey found that only 2 per cent of married people would first seek help from a marriage guidance counsellor if they had a marital problem; another found that of those who had experienced a separation, only 1 per cent had sought help from a counsellor.[85] The reality is that many people use divorce to sort their relationships out. 51 per cent of divorced men and 29 per cent of divorced women would have preferred to stay married and in 10 per cent of cases both parties wished that they had remained married. This led the authors of one study to conclude that "…many people simply do not know whether their relationship is at an end; indeed they may be using the legal system as a way of finding out."[86]

This is why the present government has been right to promote no-fault divorces in its current review of divorce law and to promote the concept of mediation, in effect allowing a year's 'cooling off' period before divorce is granted. The problem however is that free mediation services are available only to married couples. In an era of widespread cohabitation this is foolish. This is why we believe that the same rights to mediation services should be extended to all couples. Although initially very few would use it, such a 'cooling off' process might enable cohabiting couples to determine whether their problems are soluble or whether the relationship has truly broken down. It might also encourage couples to draw up cohabitation contracts to avoid costly and distressing litigation. Mediation has proved effective at resolving disagreements between couples with 80 per cent of married couples reaching some form of agreement.[87] It should be built on as a cheaper alternative to the courts.

But the failure of current policy to help cohabiting couples goes deeper than this. Although cohabitation is not yet replacing marriage, it has become a fixed part of the landscape. Cohabiting couples do not have the same rights as married couples. When a partner dies, unless a will has been made, there is no automatic right to inheritance.[88] When a relationship breaks down, strict property law principles apply to cohabiting couples whereas in the case of divorce, courts have wide discretionary powers to redistribute property and assets between partners. As a result a partner has no automatic rights to a share of property (unless there is a joint mortgage), even if their contributions to other household spending made it possible for their partner to buy their home.[89] A mother who has given up work to look after the children cannot assume that she has any financial rights to compensation.[90] In the same way cohabitants have no legal rights of occupancy unless they can prove that they have made financial contributions to the home or there is a joint tenancy agreement.[91] In many important ways the law is heavily skewed towards married couples, and, for women in particular, marriage offers the best available protection. The problem is that many cohabiting couples are ignorant about the legal no man's land that they are entering and think incorrectly that they are protected by common law. One study of long term cohabiting mothers found that just 3 out of 77 had arranged a maintenance agreement with their partners.[92] It is because of these difficulties that the Law Commission is currently reviewing property law in relation to cohabitation. In its words, "the present law is unfair, uncertain and illogical."[93]

For a younger generation there may be fewer problems. The trend towards shared financial management that we have described and the fact that more and more mortgages are joint limits one problem, as does the fact that more women are working and mothers are returning sooner to the labour market. But many cohabiting couples will still face problems if they break up – over household goods, child care and maintenance. There are also other problems for this generation. Many who benefitted from the pre-1988 advantageous mortgage tax relief for cohabitees now find themselves trapped in negative equity, having to live in the same house with their former partners. In some cases this has led to domestic violence, while in many others complex and protracted legal negotiations have been needed.

Moreover as cohabitation has spread to all classes,[94] to the extent that long term cohabiting mothers are now less likely to have formal qualifications and more likely to be poor (one in four live in no-earner households)[95] we can expect many more traditionally-minded women to suffer from relationship breakdown,[96] and from the lack of legal obligation for their partners to provide any financial support.

So far, unlike other countries, Britain has avoided tackling these issues. Yet even if many currently cohabiting couples go on to marry, we know that many of these relationships will break down, often where a child is involved, and we know that the costs of litigating property disputes can be inordinately high for the individuals concerned. A recent case took 19 days and cost the Legal Aid Fund £125,000.[97]

Policy responses to cohabitation

There are three main ways of coping with these difficulties. In the first, people would be encouraged to agree their own cohabitation contracts covering maintenance and sharing of property and finances, and insurance to provide future financial security in the event of the partner's death. Such options are currently available and have long been used in America. They are also in tune with the increasingly individualistic ethos of younger generations and with vigorous public information campaigns might be the best option for young people cohabiting today.

But there are fundamental problems with this approach. Many people cohabit not as an alternative to marriage but because they cannot afford it, are postponing it, or are apathetic about it. For precisely these reasons they are unlikely to take up contracts. Others by contrast will find the idea of a cohabitation contract clinical and unromantic. But the biggest problem is that so many people are ignorant about their rights. Without an extremely vigorous information campaign it is hard to imagine behaviour changing.

The second option, proposed by many on the right, is to reinforce marriage through fiscal means. Marriage is seen as the central socialising institution of society which has been consistently under-valued and undermined. We should support it because it is better at creating stable relationships and because there is a general public interest in keeping couples together.

Analysts like Patricia Morgan[98] argue that economic tools – above all the incentives and penalties built into tax and benefits – are vital to reinforcing marriage. Our own analysis, however, suggests this is increasingly less likely to be the case, and that an excessively economistic analysis can be misleading. In the first place it is hard to explain why women initiate the great majority of divorces when it is they who tend to lose out most economically. This is why the criticisms of the tapering of the married tax allowance since 1990 and the advocacy of a return to an index-linked married couples tax allowance alongside tougher penalties for unmarried lone parents, are unconvincing. In any case, the rise in divorce and cohabitation long preceded the freezing of the married couples tax allowance.

Reinforcing marriage through fiscal means looks unlikely to reverse behaviour. The only detailed study of long term cohabiting mothers conducted in this country found that the three main reasons why they had not married were the fear of divorce, the high cost of weddings and their objection to the institution of marriage itself. No one cited the absence of fiscal incentives.[99] Those cohabiting mothers who would like to marry but do not because of the cost, are more likely to have an unemployed partner, are themselves more likely to have no qualifications, and are less likely to be in paid work. They are therefore unlikely to qualify for the married couples tax allowance anyway.

Another flaw of this analysis is the presumption that marriage will in itself lead to greater stability. In fact, as we have seen, research consistently shows that married couples who have cohabited are more likely to divorce than couples who marry before living together.

The third option is to follow countries such as Sweden, Canada and Australia in minimising the penalties against cohabiting couples. In Sweden, if a couple is judged to be in a 'marriage-like relationship' (something which is not defined in statute but rather left to the discretion of the courts which generally take five years as a rule of thumb) the law gives cohabiting couples interests in each other's assets as well as providing some special rules in the event of a death of partner.[100] In New South Wales, partners can apply to the court for a 'property adjustment order' if they have lived as a couple for at least two years, and they can claim compensation, particularly if they have been in a 'homemaker' role.[101] In Canada individuals can make claims on assets and goods up to one year after a break up.[102] In Britain similar approaches are being suggested, for example by the Scottish Law Commission.[103]

Reforming the law to give cohabiting couples similar rights (and thus responsibilities) to married couples is inevitably controversial. Many fear that to do so would undermine marriage when it needs propping up. Others fear that it would undermine the freedom of people who have deliberately chosen not to marry.[104]

In our view, however, the effectiveness of marriage is best achieved by enabling people to develop long term relationships of commitment, not by penalising those couples who are to all intents and purposes in marriage-like relationships. The same principles should apply to cohabiting couples (including gay couples) as to married couples, where they are considered to be in a marriage-like relationship. Women in particular should be able to claim for the economic disadvantage of looking after children (or for that matter helping out in a family business), even if we stop short of full rights to maintenance. Following the experience of other countries we suggest that the definition of a 'marriage like relationship' should be determined by the courts on a range of criteria (length of relationship, whether a child is involved or not, and whether the relationship is sexually active) rather than through the statute book.

Many will see this as an illiberal imposition of marriage-like obligations onto couples who might have a principled opposition to the institution itself. For this reason we propose that cohabiting couples should be able to jointly opt out of these provisions at all points in the relationship, except when a child is involved.

Reforms of this kind will not solve the problem of relationship breakdown. But they may contribute to a culture in which people think harder about their commitments.

Clearly many people would like to make all cohabitees get married. But this is not likely to happen. Even if it did it wouldn't make their relationships any more stable. Instead the policy priority is to bring clear rules to the substantial minority who are, and will remain, outside marriage and thus in an important sense outside the law.

The new parentalism

By far the greatest problems resulting from unstable relationships are those involving children. However much personal relationships should be a private matter, when children are involved the state is bound to have a role. In recent years there have been important advances. The Children's Act and the Child Support Agency have been crucial in helping to define children's rights and parents' responsibilities. The focus on children has helped to clear away much of the ideological undergrowth that surrounds so many debates about the family, to better focus on the real choices and interests at stake in an age when parenthood and marriage are no longer so intimately linked.

Parental rights and responsibilities for cohabitees
But despite these achievements, there remain important problems. In the past policy makers could assume that marriage was the institution through which parents' rights and responsibilities towards children could be defined. Today, however, a third of children are born outside marriage. Most of these are born to parents in committed relationships (the number of joint registrations on the birth of a child amongst unmarried parents has been growing steadily since 1982).[105] But there are major discrepancies for cohabiting couples.

Whilst the Child Support Act clearly stated in law that cohabiting fathers and absent fathers are financially responsible for their children, they do not have any parallel rights to bring up the child. Many wrongly assume that by jointly registering the birth of the child, each parent shares rights and responsibilities. But in reality it is the mother alone who has exclusive rights.

As we have seen many cohabiting couples are ignorant of the law. Few fathers are given formal rights and responsibilities, and in one study fewer than ten percent of cohabiting mothers had made a will naming their partner as the guardian of the child in the event of their death.[106] Many point to the fact that the absence of fathers' rights only really becomes a problem for cohabiting couples if the relationship breaks down or if the partner dies. It is only then that many fathers become aware that they lack basic parental rights to access or custody.[107] Opponents of reform argue that men can already opt in to rights, either through a court order and, since the Children's Act, through a less bureaucratic Parental Responsibility Agreement.

However this argument against reform does not address the issue of fairness. It ignores the inconsistency of the state's treatment of cohabiting fathers, conferring financial responsibility without automatic parallel rights, and it assumes that women should be the sole carer. A better approach would be to confer parental rights and responsibilities automatically. Rather than an opt-in system we would favour an opt-out system in the case of joint registration of the birth of the child, which could only be revoked if the mother and father chose to renounce their rights.[108]

Cohabiting couples should also be able to adopt a child. Currently they have to apply individually for adoption which makes the legal position of the other adoptive parent unclear: they cannot apply as a couple.[109] The recent White Paper, *Divorce and the Future*, still makes a strong presumption in favour of married couples and continues to exclude cohabiting couples. This straightforward inequity should be addressed: the main criterion should be the qualities, not the legal status, of the prospective parents.[110]

We also believe that the state should now clearly set out the legal responsibilities of parents to a child. Currently the Children's Act and the Child Support Act spell out some of these, but as we have shown this varies between married and unmarried fathers and more importantly there is no clear cut overall statement mapping parental responsibilities. Such a statement could be provided to all parents automatically when births are registered.

Children as private or public goods
The bigger problem, however, is that public policy has neither been consistent nor effective. Over the last ten years, despite a popular rhetoric of family values, many young families have become worse off, whilst the relative status of pensioners has improved. The numbers of families with dependent children below the poverty line has increased dramatically, both because of deteriorating labour market conditions[111] and because of relationship breakdown. At the same time the absurdities of an unintegrated tax and benefits system mean that there are clear disincentives to work: a married father with two children today can earn only 35 per cent of average manual earnings before he has to pay tax, compared to 101 per cent in 1950.[112] Having a child costs money. Yet compared to other countries, the weight of fiscal policy does little to help most parents. We don't subsidise child care through direct provision or through tax breaks (except marginally), and unlike many other countries in Europe we don't have a system of parental leave. Child benefit is low (partly because it is universal). The CSA, which might have been expected to put children's needs first has instead become primarily a means for the state to contain rising social security costs, involving a further shift in the burden of costs from those without children to parents.

Unlike other countries we do not put a value on the parenting role. The drift of policy seems to be towards treating children as private goods – whose costs should be borne solely by their parents – rather than public goods whose cost should be shared more widely. In our view this is neither philosophically nor politically sustainable. Today's children are tomorrow's workers and parents and the investment that we make today will pay dividends in the long run.

Already the problems with the existing approach are becoming clear. For some the over-emphasis on personal fulfilment at work has become corrosive. Amitai Etzioni criticises the egoism of dual earner couples who pursue careers at the expense of their children.[113] He has analysed the resulting parenting deficit which began at the time of the industrial revolution when men left the home to go to work, but which has been exacerbated by the entry of women into the labour market in unprecedented numbers over the last two decades.

Other factors are converging to heighten this deficit. Women are now returning much sooner to the labour market. In 1979 only a quarter of women returned to work within nine months of giving birth; by 1988 this proportion was 50 per cent[114] and by 1989 it was two women in three.[115] The combination of long working hours – the average British working week is an hour longer than in 1983 – and more women working means that people's time for family activities has been squeezed. Between 1988 and 1994 those agreeing that 'I never have enough time to get things done' rose from 52 per cent to 57 per cent. Amongst full-time female workers, an astonishing 86 per cent agreed with this statement.[116] Our own qualitative research has confirmed that many feel they are working harder than ever before, whether as professionals trying to establish a career, or on the shopfloor.

Etzioni's analysis has challenged an older generation of feminists for whom encouraging women into the workplace to give them financial independence and an identity beyond motherhood has been a central plank of the equality strategy. They fear that his analysis gives ammunition to those who want women to return to the home while men remain as breadwinners, even though he has been explicit that both parents have a duty to tackle the parenting deficit.[117] Our research shows just how much working fathers and mothers want to spend more time with the family, how much they feel guilty about not being able to spend sufficient time with their children and how uneasy they feel about the poor quality of child care available.

Committed and involved parenting means that children grow up more securely attached than those whose parenting has been sporadic and uneven.[118] For young boys in particular the presence of a father is crucial in helping them to define themselves positively rather than simply negatively, by rejecting the image of the mother.[119]

Fortunately, there is growing evidence that young men want to be more actively involved in parenting. Many regret the lack of involvement that they had with their own father, and are aware of what Charlie Lewis and Margaret O'Brien call the 'paradox of patriarchy', namely that "while a father may be 'head' of his family ... he is constrained from being a central character within it."[120] At the same time working mothers, despite all the stresses and strains of modern motherhood are still happier than non-working mothers and, as our own research has shown, are prepared to pay for the privilege of working by directly paying for child care.

Government policy now needs to help young couples to parent effectively, within the context of a changed culture. It needs to indicate that it values parenting, but in a new way that involves fathers as well as mothers.

One simple means by which this could be done would be to end the married couples tax allowance and to refocus allowances (perhaps limited to basic rate) to couples with children. There is certainly no longer any justification for special fiscal treatment for married couples as opposed to cohabiting couples; indeed social security law already ignores the distinction. There is also a strong case for parental allowances (as in Australia). These have been proposed to remove the disincentives to

91

taking a job for members of no-earner couples, by giving an allowance to whoever looks after the children even if their partner gets a job.[121]

But as important will be new rights to ease parental leave (for both men and women), a series of detailed models of which are currently being developed by Demos, alongside a strategy for child care.[122]

Any child care strategy should not in our view rely solely on formal organisations, although there is much to be done to improve their quality. It would be wrong to offer fiscal support to childcare which discriminated against friends, neighbours and family members, who may be better placed to provide it. A survey for Age Concern found that grandparents are already playing a vital role in helping parents: eight out of ten younger grandparents (45-54) had babysat or childminded in the previous six months.[123] One radical option would be to provide childcare vouchers so that they could be paid to grandparents or other proxies as well as to accredited organisations. This could be devised as a component of a Community Service for Old People. Despite the policing problems involved, a policy of this kind might have long-term advantages, not least in re-engaging the extended family.

We should also consider more radical options. One is to ensure that in the case of divorce or separation, family assets should be divided three ways, with the third part (whose size would depend on the age and number of children) going to the custodial parent, usually the mother. Another is to provide special training credits for parents who take time off work, either by going part-time or by taking a period of full-time parenting.

There is no more basic obligation for any society than that of creating and bringing up successor generations. We need a new approach to parenting, a new form of parentalism, which concentrates on addressing children's needs while also enabling both fathers and mothers to achieve a better balance between work and family life. And we need to do so in ways that still enable women to work – because otherwise growing numbers will simply opt out of parenting.

The policy implications for today's 18-34 year olds are stark. When they grow old a long-term failure to keep reproducing will leave too few workers there to support them. Britain would therefore do well to learn from the experience of other countries which have found that whereas in the past there may have seemed to be an inherent conflict between women's equality and initiatives to boost the family, now the two can go hand in hand. In Norway for example, women's position has been greatly strengthened not by extensive childcare but rather by ensuring generous paid leave – and leave to look after sick children.[124] Sweden, whose parental leave scheme is the most generous in Europe, also has the second highest birth rate next to Ireland. In both cases equality has advanced in tandem with 'pro-natalism'.

The care deficit and the sandwich generation

Reforms of this kind might go some way towards confronting the parenting deficit. But this generation also faces the prospect of being sandwiched between the care needs of children and of their elderly parents. Nearly one in three people who care for the sick, elderly or handicapped for more than 20 hours a week also have children under the age of 16 to care for.[125] These care pressures are being compounded by demographics: as our society ages, there are insufficient carers available. This is a long term trend. In 1900 for every person aged over 85 there were 24 women in their 50s (the group which carries out most informal care); by 2000 there will be only three.[126] The impact of these shifts is already being felt,[127] but it will intensify as the crisis in long term residential care deepens and as the state continues to pass the burden back out on to the family itself.[128]

Moral persuasion will not be enough to solve this problem: middle aged women will increasingly refuse to sacrifice their freedom or career to care for the old.

93

Instead, new economic mechanisms will be needed. Germany, whose inter-generational pressures are more severe than Britain, offers one intriguing model. The state has consistently required that families care and pay for the elderly.[129] Until recently if families didn't do this, legislation allowed social security officials to access bank details of family members and force them to contribute to the cost of care for elderly relatives.

However, since 1994, they have exacted a compulsory national levy on earnings to pay for universal long term care insurance. This amounts to 1 per cent of earnings in 1995 rising to 1.7 per cent in 1996.[130]

In Britain, it is worth considering a model of this kind.[131] However unlike the German scheme which builds in incentives to encourage family members – nearly always women – to care through cash assistance, we would advocate building incentives the reverse way round so that reliance upon formal care outside the family setting is encouraged.[132] So whereas in the case of childcare we may need to shift resources towards the extended family, policies for eldercare should not mirror this. One reason is that old people are themselves uncomfortable about depending on their children,[133] but perhaps more importantly, the flaw of the German scheme is that it will encourage inadequate and medically inappropriate care, which is potentially far more dangerous for the elderly than for children.[134]

Modernising marriage

Much of what has been said thus far might seem to suggest that marriage is a dying institution and that policy should no longer prop it up. In fact our view is that marriage needs to be modernised, not abandoned. But this can only be done if we recognise that marriage isn't working. As an institution it has not been adequately modernised. This failure begins with the ceremony. More and more people want to personalise their own marriage ceremony and claim it as their own. In our survey, 61 per cent of women aged between 18-34 and 67 per cent of men aged between 18-34 practically never attend religious services compared to 39 per cent of women over 55 and 61 per cent of men over 55, with women's values changing the most dramatically. But marriage rituals don't easily cater for people's own (frequently secular) values. Today most people marry not to mark the beginning of a life together but rather as an important staging post in lives that are already shared.

The churches have been slow to adapt. Many feel that the ceremony has lost meaning, partly because so many vows made in front of God have been broken, partly because the idea of the white wedding clashes with a culture where premarital sex is the norm, and partly because the vows themselves seem rigid, dry and dusty. To our knowledge the Unitarian Church is alone in allowing experimentation with the rewriting of the marriage vows (though even here it has to be within legal limits). The result is that for many, and not only agnostics and atheists, church weddings are empty rituals (and this isn't helped by the CoE's uneasy relationship with cohabiting couples).[135] This is surely one reason why the majority of marriages are now civil.[136]

Yet register's offices seem antiseptic and bureaucratic, like a visit to the tax office or the DSS rather than the place to make one of the most important commitments in your life. The recent liberalisation of the 200 year old marriage regulations which now allow people to wed in 'approved places' such as hotels or the Royal Pavilion at Brighton is a step in the right direction, but it still severely limits where people get married. There are still far more places where you can't marry than where you can. You can't for example have even a civil marriage in your own home, outdoors, in your favourite park, on your favourite hill or beach. Nor is there much choice about who conducts the ceremony.

What solutions are on offer? How can marriage be modernised and made more popular? In our view marriage needs to be deregulated. Elsewhere, marriage has been liberalised. Canada and Australia have thousands of 'celebrants' (people licensed to marry people). In Australia they are listed in the Yellow Pages and in Canada you can get a marriage licence in your local shopping mall. Further liberalisation of the marriage regulations – by allowing other people to be licensed as marriage-makers as well as religious representatives or officials of the state – might prove popular amongst a generation which likes to do things in its own way. Liberalisation would also provide an opportunity to extend marriage to gay couples many of whom want a more formal, legal symbol of commitment.[137]

Liberalisation would return marriage to individuals, from whose hands it was wrested in 1753 by Lord Hardwicke's Marriage Act. It would also open up many possibilities, both for a more personal style of marriage and for greater commercialisation. The funeral supermarkets in France (soon set to come to Britain) could be joined by marriage supermarkets. One might imagine ceremonies at Marks and Spencer or Centerparks. Romantics would no longer need to fly to Las Vegas. Liberalisation would legitimise the cottage industry of 'marriage makers' who are already helping people to devise their own rituals and ceremonies in spite of the state. And competition might also reduce prices in the marriage market, so that fewer people would be put off by the cost.

Far from being the final nail in marriage's coffin, modernisation might be the best way to save marriage as a mainstream institution. Indeed, the next few years may be set to bring a reinvention of many of the rituals of commitment. The Humanist Association, arts groups such as Welfare State International and Michael Young's Family Covenant Association are all developing alternative ceremonies not just for marriage but also for birth and death, but they lack the legal authority to marry people or to conduct birth naming ceremonies. The Family Covenant Association is also encouraging people to agree a Covenant setting out their commitments to a child.[138] In the years ahead we will need more new rituals of this kind, even perhaps for divorce and relationship breakdown, since good relations with former partners can contribute a lot to a happy life.

Conclusion

The driving forces behind the changes in relationships and family life are the combination of consumerism, a changing labour market and a more open democratic culture of opportunity. These forces are profound and show no signs of being reversed.

They have also been far more powerful than the influence of the state, which has tended to follow society rather than to lead. Attempts to blame the state for stepping in as the 'proxy' male, subsidising lone parents and penalising married couples,[139] and the portrayal of this generation as Saturn's (ie the state's) children, are misleading.[140] Capitalism and individualism have been far more powerful engines of change than the state.

But the main lesson to be drawn from this chapter is that most of the mainstream policy ideas being promoted around marriage and the family are really dealing with effects rather than underlying causes. Because they ignore the ways in which values are changing, they are unlikely to work. They are either sticking plasters too marginal to have any effect, or instruments so blunt that they cannot hope to be legitimate. In the long-run our best hope is to enable people to make better relationships, and to negotiate them better, all within a clear, and clearly fair, framework of legal rights and responsibilities.

Reconnecting politics

For many young people in Britain today politics has become something of a dirty word. People under 25 are four times less likely to be registered[1] than any other age group, less likely to vote for or join a political party, and less likely to be politically active.[2] Only 6 per cent of 15-34 year olds describe themselves as 'very interested in politics'.[3]

Voting and political activism (%)

	Age			
	18-24	25-34	35-54	55yrs+
Voted at last election[a]	43	68	77	82
Political activism[b]				
Women	3	10	17	11
Men	9	13	24	15

[a]Source: MORI (Base, 1960)
[b]Source: Socioconsult (Base, 2034)

Their disconnection shows a consistent pattern. The young are less active than the old, women less than men, ethnic minority groups less than the white majority, and the poor less than the rich.[4] Our *Socioconsult* analysis shows that ABC1 men in the age range are four times more likely to be active politically than C2DE men, while ABC1 women are nine times as likely to be active as C2DE women. The aversion to politics is – oddly enough – strongest amongst the very groups that might be expected to gain most from it. This aversion also affects views of politics as a career. Far from seeing the job of an MP or Prime Minister as the very pinnacle of achievement, one recent survey of young people found politics the least popular career choice of any on offer.[5]

The overwhelming story emerging from our research, both quantitative and qualitative, is of an historic political disconnection. In effect, an entire generation has opted out of party politics.

Some attribute this solely to the peculiarities of the British parliamentary system, or to having one party in power for so long. But these patterns are not peculiar to Britain. There are parallels in almost every industrialised country. In Germany there is mounting concern about falling political participation: a recent survey found young people are 50 per cent less likely to join parties, and whilst there was a 77.5 per cent turnout rate in the 1990 Bundestag elections, amongst people aged 18-25 the rate dropped to just 62.5 per cent.[6] France too has been exercised by youth alienation: former President Mitterand was so concerned that he commissioned a poll of the views of France's 15-25 year olds (and, ironically, proceeded to alienate them further by the manner in which the poll was carried out.)[7]

In Australia an official report on young people's attitudes to voting concluded that "The single most important reason why young people fail to register to vote is because they do not see any direct link between the Government or Government institutions and their own lives......The same apathy is responsible for their failure to acquire any real political knowledge, leading many young people to feel incapable of recording a meaningful vote."[8]

In America there has been concern about youth apathy ever since 18 year olds first got the vote in 1972.

18-20 year olds, who started out with a low turnout, dropped a further 15 points between 1972 and 1988. Even with a slight upturn for the 1992 Presidential election, average voter turnout amongst young people was only 37 per cent and the age gap in participation widened from 20 points in 1964 to 35 points in 1988,[9] leading analysts to conclude that "political leaders are not only failing to impart citizenship values, they are actually alienating young people from public life"[10] Others damningly conclude that "today's young Americans, aged 18-30, know less and care less about news and public affairs than any other generation of Americans in the past 50 years."[11] In Canada, too, one poll found that 18-21 year olds were three times less likely to vote than those aged over 50.[12]

Some might dismiss these trends as symptoms of a youth culture which people grow out of – the political equivalents of MTV and Beavis and Butthead. Unfortunately the figures do not bear them out. Instead the evidence suggests that young people are leading a deepening public detachment from politics.

For example in the UK the number of people who express dissatisfaction with the way Parliament is working has doubled in four years since 1991.[13] Trust in societies' core institutions has steadily fallen, leaving national government (at 15 per cent), and local government (at 25 per cent) receiving only minority support.[14] At the ballot box too, while abstentions have risen, governments have been elected with ever smaller shares of electoral support.[15]

For the parties the process of detachment and hollowing out has been steady and cumulative. The Conservative party now has only one member for every three it had when Margaret Thatcher took power, and every six it had in the 1950s. It has fewer qualified local agents than at any time since the late 1940s.[16] The party has also found it difficult to bring in fresh blood. Membership of the Young Conservatives is reportedly down to 7,500 or less and there have been rumours that they may be wound up.[7] As a result the average age of a Conservative member is over 61[18] and almost half are over 66. Only 5 per cent are younger than 35.[19]

Labour, which historically has had fewer members than the Conservatives, has experienced similar pressures. Since the 1950s its membership has fallen from nearly a million to an all time low of 265,000 in 1988.[20] Research in 1992[21] found that the average age of Labour members was 48, and a 1993 report, *The New Generation*, pointed out that there were more than three times as many Labour party members over 66 as under 25 and concluded that the Labour party "relies heavily on older members for local campaigning and suffers from the absence at local level of active and enthusiastic young members"[22] Historically of course Labour has relied on unions to provide it with a steady base of membership but this source has dried up.[23] Moreover, high rates of youth unemployment, and the weak union presence in the places young people work, mean that the workplace is no longer a prime recruiting ground.[24] The latest official figures suggest that Labour has increased its membership by one third to 346,000 since Tony Blair became leader, with most of the new recruits under 40.[25] Its Youth Section (15-26 year olds) has increased its membership in the past 18 months from 14,000 to 22,000, meaning that the average age for Labour does seem to be falling.[26] But these figures still represent a very small youth membership by historical standards, whether those of the Young Conservatives (who once had well over half a million members) or continental socialist parties.

The traditional women's organisations have suffered a parallel decline. The National Federation of Women's Institutes membership has fallen from 467,000 in 1945 to 299,000 in 1992 and membership of the Mother's Union and the National Union of Townswomen's Guilds halved between 1971-92.[27] These organisations have an ageing and declining membership,[28] partly because so many women have gone into the workforce.

One might expect new feminist organisations to be recruiting these lost members.[29] Instead Demos' qualitative research amongst these organisations found that many are extremely concerned to find younger members,[30] but "younger women seem less likely to see the need for or benefit of women's groups and do not seem to feel as strongly about the need for social change in the area of gender".[31] Similar concerns have been expressed about the dependence of the major green organisations on a middle-aged membership.

The switched off generation?

It is easy to paint a very negative picture. The evidence seems to suggest that 18-34 year olds are apathetic and inward looking: that those at the lower end of the age range have not yet fully accepted the responsibilities of adulthood whilst those at the higher end of the age range have simply become selfish. While young people are quick to assert their rights, our survey found that just 49 per cent of people aged between 18-34 say they are willing to sacrifice some individual freedom in the public interest as compared to 61.5 per cent of people aged between 35-54 and 64.5 per cent of people aged over 55 – a clear sign that political disconnection is linked to a wider social disconnection.

Political involvement and alienation (% agree)

		Age		
		18-34	35-54	55yrs+
In general the people in	Women	22	27	45
charge know best	Men	28	35	53
I'm not interested in politics	Women	55	49	47
	Men	45	39	42

Source:Socioconsult (Base, 2034)

However this image could be misleading. Young people do care strongly about certain issues. Environmentalism, famine, animal rights and health issues such as AIDS excite commitment in a way that traditional politics does not.[32] In one recent survey 73 per cent supported helping the homeless, 71 per cent greater rights for the disabled, followed by support for the NHS and animal rights at 66 per cent and 64 per cent respectively. Interestingly too, 56 per cent support single parents and 50 per cent women's right to an abortion.[33] Recently youth politics has regained its visibility, with protests on roads at Twyford Down or veal calves at Brightlingsea. The campaign against the Criminal Justice Bill has even led some to proclaim a new era of youth activism.

In the same way although young women are reluctant to identity with the feminist label they share – probably more than ever – the aims and values of the women's movement. A recent poll confirmed our own qualitative research findings: 71 per cent of women felt positively about feminism and 49 per cent thought that it had been good for both men and women.[34]

Given the right issue young people do become active. Although our *Socioconsult* analysis suggests that young people are less environmentally active than the 35-55 age group, environmental concerns are much more likely to galvanise them into action than anything else. Women aged between 18-34 are almost five times as likely (and men three times as likely) to be active on the environment as on other issues.[35] Younger women's strong interest in environmental activism also helps to explain the relative success of organisations such as the Women's Environmental Network which have blended a form of eco-feminism with practical action.[36]

This focused activism is particularly striking in relation to animals. Remarkably, a third of young people claim to have been involved in protests on animal rights, and over a quarter of 15-21 year olds sympathise with protests which risk causing damage to buildings or other property on behalf of animal rights.[37]

There also seems to be an appeal (at least to a minority) when politics brings with it a lifestyle as in the case of the 'new age travellers' movement[38] or the rave scene:[39] symptoms of a broader commitment to self-discovery that is manifest in the fact that 96 per cent of

103

18-34 year olds agree that 'everyone has to find out for themselves what sort of life they want to lead.' Young people, in other words, seem far more predisposed to single issues, to issues where they can have an immediate effect, and perhaps to 'life' issues rather than social or economic ones.[40]

There is also some evidence that younger generations have become more willing to protest.[41] Public tolerance for illegal demonstrations has risen over the last decade with 68 per cent now agreeing that there are times when protesters are justified in breaking the law, an increase of 14 per cent since 1984.[42] None of this may add up to all that much – certainly the capacity of the new forms of politics to achieve far-reaching change seems limited. But these examples are important qualifications to the picture of a wholly apathetic generation.

The sources of disconnection from mainstream politics

Why then are people turning off traditional politics despite their evident concern about specific issues? Why is a generation which is more educated than its parents less active when available research on voting patterns shows that the more educated you are, the more likely you are to vote?

There are a variety of general explanations. Some focus on the declining power of politics or the nation state in the face of globalisation. Another explanation is that we have simply become too busy. Our time has for various reasons become squeezed. Democracy takes a great deal of time and its forms have scarcely been modernised (unlike work and leisure), so that the relative appeal of investing time in it has diminished. This is certainly the case with middle class women who formed the base for the Conservative and Liberal parties, and for much of the voluntary sector, and who are now much more likely to be devoting their energies to their jobs,[43] particularly younger women.[44]

But the most commonly used explanation is that

people are generally satisfied: with greater material affluence there is simply no need to campaign. A general culture of contentment leads many of us to choose to spend our time doing pleasurable things rather than campaigning to bring about social or political change. Life opportunities far beyond those imaginable a couple of generations ago diminish the appeal of dusty meeting halls, resolutions and fetes.

Dimensions of discontent

But how credible is the argument that at root it is satisfaction and complacency that explain the detachment from politics?

Discontent with the core institutions
The first reason for doubting this is the evidence of the extent to which people are cynical about the institutions with power – whether government or business or indeed any other organisations that are seen as part of 'them'.[45] This deep seated rejection of society's central institutions has gathered pace with each successive generation. Our *Socioconsult* survey suggests that the shift away from tradition and the decline of deference really begins in the 35-55 year old age group, but is steadily deepening with younger age groups who are fast losing respect for, and even interest in, the people in charge

These general patterns are stark enough. But amongst subgroups the detachment is particularly striking – notably single mothers and young women aged between 15-17, a majority of whom agree that 'it will always be impossible to reform the system enough, we need to close most of it down and start afresh'.

Frustrated ambition
The second reason for doubting the contentment thesis is the evidence of frustrated ambitions. Our survey finds that some 38 per cent of the population feel frustrated in some way. Within the 18-34 age range, lower income groups feel especially frustrated (48 per cent of C2DEs)

as do single parents and non-workers. The revolution in women's lives means that many women lower down the class scale now aspire to personal fulfilment at work as well as at home. Indeed the levels of frustration amongst C1 and C2 women should be a warning against any complacency: clearly expectations have been raised and not met.

Gender discontent
The third dimension of discontent is gender. 30 years after the most recent wave of feminism began power structures remain overwhelmingly male. There is very strong support for policy changes – such as affordable high quality childcare – but little sign of their happening. Within firms, although women are advancing, the pace is too slow for many. But part of the problem here is the double disconnection; although women feel aggrieved they identify only weakly with women's organisations, and sometimes see the women's movement image as unattractive and man-hating.

Hostility to the system and the nation
But perhaps the most striking trend is the extent to which many young people now take pride in being out of the system. In the table opposite we have aggregated responses to a number of statements: agreement with the statements 'I do not feel that I'm part of the British system and I'm proud of it' and 'if I had the chance I would emigrate' and disagreement with the statements 'I feel that I really belong to this neighbourhood' and 'on the whole I prefer to buy British'. The result is a 'disconnection index' which shows just how much young people feel detached from British society.

This pride in being out of the system is not just a product of greater inequality or lifestage. Young singles, newly weds and single parents score identically on it; full-time workers actually score above average; and attachment is unrelated to income level. This value would seem to be firmly embedded – one version of an

Disconnection index (%)

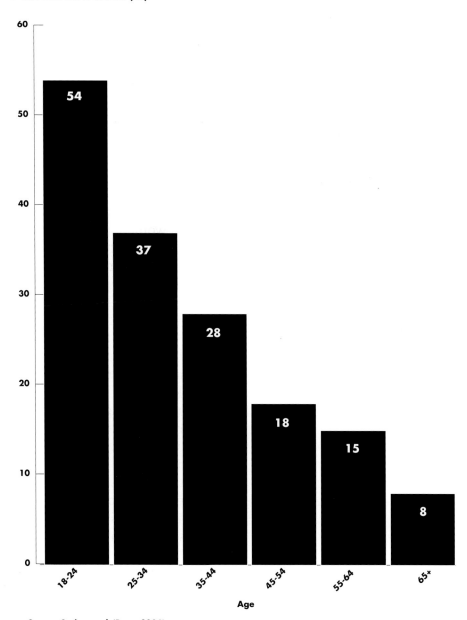

Source: *Socioconsult* (Base, 2034)

individualism which is gaining a wider currency. It is no accident that those people who are proud to be out of the system are also likely to be attached to other more anti-social values such as crude hedonism, being willing to take risks, living on the edge or taking pleasure in violence. Unsurprisingly perhaps those who are proud to be out of the system are also the least optimistic. Perhaps whereas in the past the anger of people feeling excluded from the system was directed into radical political movements, in the 90s such anger is as likely to manifest itself in the rising number of girl gangs on the streets of Britain's cities, in aimless rioting or hedonistic joy riding.

Generation on the edge

So on one level we find great disillusionment with party politics and a fatalistic approach to whether problems can be solved. On another level we see that young people do care deeply about certain issues and are far from contented.[46] How will these attitudes influence politics?

It is certainly possible to describe pessimistic scenarios. The disconnection we have analysed could easily escalate, with a further unravelling of political allegiance, and growing conflicts between the sexes and the generations. Greater individualism, instead of fostering responsibility, may make people ever more selfish: less willing to sacrifice their personal freedom for the collective good, more mindful of their rights and less willing to accept their wider social responsibilities.

The rise of the underwolf?
One of the dimensions of conflict looks likely to be a more volatile politics of exclusion which no longer has the structures of class and labour movement politics to provide direction. The economic and social pressures towards exclusion are increasing, at the same time as values are making it more acceptable to behave in aggressive antisocial ways. The underdogs look set to

bite back ever more – perhaps we should call them underwolves. They take pride in being out of the system and flouting its rules, and their position is set to be one of the dominant issues on the public agenda, whether from the perspective of tackling the causes of exclusion or coping with its effects.

Sex wars?

The second dimension of potential conflict is that between the sexes. There are some worrying signs that we could see an escalation of the sex war. In the USA, there are now far more assertive movements of men's rights, in conflict with women who are equally assertive of their hard-won rights. In Britain this looks less likely, and if anything gender is becoming less visible on the public agenda, not least because the economic divisions between women and between men are more striking. Converging values may also contain the more extreme potential clashes.

Intergenerational conflict?

The third dimension of potential conflict is intergenerational. In the EU there are 4.5 workers to every pensioner. By 2020 this will have shrunk to 4 in Britain; 3.5 in France; and 3 in Germany.[47] In Europe as a whole 50 years ago people over 65 made up just one in fourteen of the community's population compared to one in five today. This demographic revolution has occurred because of the combination of rising longevity (a child born in 1990 may expect to live almost 10 years longer than one born in 1950) and a declining birthrate, as the average number of children born to each woman in Europe has fallen from 2.63 in 1960 to 1.87 in 1980.[48]

The OECD has been particularly pessimistic, arguing that "under existing regulations the evolution of public pension schemes is likely to put a heavy and increasing burden on the working population in coming decades. Such a financial strain may put inter-generational solidarity, a concept on which all public retirement pensions are based, at risk."[49] More recently the International Labour Organisation warned that welfare expenditure on the rising numbers of elderly threatens to cripple Western industrialised economies unless radical action is taken. Public pension expenditure is predicted to become the largest budget item for most industrialised countries during the next decade.[50]

Signs of impending conflict are certainly visible. In New Zealand it has been claimed that the 'welfare generation' has 'captured' the welfare state and steered it from being a youth orientated state to one directed towards older people.[51] In America a poll found that only 9 per cent of Americans aged between 18-34 believe that the social security system will have adequate funds to provide their retirement benefits (as Newt Gingrich pointed out this is fewer than the proportion who believe they will meet an extra-terrestrial in their lifetime) and 83 per cent believe that the Government has made financial promises that it cannot keep.[52]

The organisation 'Lead...or Leave', which claims some 20,000 members, and is supported by Ross Perot,[53] has been quick to capitalise on the disillusionment of American twenty-somethings. They have organised demonstrations against pensioners' groups, their leaders encourage young people to burn their social security cards and they ask why the young should pay for the profligacy of previous generations. Other 'post partisan' organisations include Third Millennium, which was set up to "represent and express the generational concerns of Americans born between 1961 and 1981", and advances generational politics on issues ranging from social security spending to protecting the environment.[54]

There are real grievances behind these organisations. Recent figures from the Committee for a Responsible Federal Budget show that entitlements for the elderly already represent 35 per cent of the total federal budget. And their calculations show that Newt Gingrich's budget plans would increase the share of the budget going to the elderly to 43 per cent by the year 2002.[55]

Perhaps the best picture of this inter-generational shift was suggested by the social philosopher Daniel Callaghan. The typical small town in mid-America, he suggests, now has a shiny hospital and a dilapidated school, a symptom of the way in which future generations are being bled dry to finance the old.[56]

Is wealth cascading up the generations?

Fortunately, the demographic and political basis for a breakdown of the social contract is less evident in Britain than elsewhere. Our demographic prospects are not as stark as those in Germany, Japan or France. But even so, it would be wrong to underestimate the scope for problems.

A first attempt at generational auditing found that over the last decade the proportion of the retired population receiving incomes below the official poverty line had fallen substantially at the same time as the numbers of families with dependent children had increased,[57] a problem which has been compounded by the problems of negative equity amongst younger people.

Grey power looks set to increasingly dominate leisure and consumer spending.[58] Well Off Older People, the 'Whoopie generation', are enjoying a prosperous old age,[59] while people in their 40s and 50s have enjoyed the good luck of sustained growth and rising house prices and are likely to further redefine old age as an opportunity to travel and experiment.[60]

Governments all over the world are having to absorb the demands of the powerful grey lobby. Whereas 20 years ago it was unions that governments feared most, now, by a nice historical irony, Jack Jones, the most famous union leader of them all, is heading a pensioners movement with the potential power to make ministers sweat. The first Pensioners Parliament was held in 1995, calling for a minimum state pension, equivalent to a third of the weekly average wage.

Bearing in mind the 'age interest' nature of politics in the USA a recent survey asked older people if they would join a political party which would specifically further their interests; a significant minority (over one fifth) in Britain and in Europe said that they would.[61]

But whilst today's pensioners may feel hard done by things look even bleaker for those coming after them. Projected income figures from the Henley Centre's Planning for Social Change programme indicate that the 20 something generation are financially worse off than preceding generations and face the prospect of declining real incomes. Our own analysis of the British Household Panel Study finds that nearly four times as many 16-34 year olds are in negative equity as older generations and many more are in debt, partly because of the costs of going through higher education.[62] Henley conclude that "if the plight of the new generation, relative to that of its parents, becomes more widely understood it is quite conceivable that pressure on the older generation to make its share of sacrifices – and to sustain the middle class ideal of its children – will intensify".[63] John Hills, an economist at the LSE in a study of intergenerational equity[64] finds that it is Jack Jones' generation and those over 70 who have benefitted most from the welfare state, putting in less than they are now taking out. If, as is likely, benefits such as pensions fail to keep up with earnings, people aged between 18-34 may get the worst of all worlds – higher taxes to pay for the old, but no guarantees that there will be adequate pensions or long-term care for them.[65] Far from wealth cascading down the generations, as John Major promised, the flow may be going in the reverse direction.

Some academics have argued that although the seeds of inter-generational conflict were sown by the current Government's decision in the 1980s to cut future pensions by removing the link to earnings[66] the continuing strength of intergenerational solidarity is proof that the old social contract can be restored: 45.9 per cent, for example, strongly agree that people in employment have a duty to ensure through contributions or taxes that older people have a decent standard of living, with only 3.1 per cent disagreeing strongly.[67] Research by McCann Erickson on European Generation X finds that despite uncertainties about the future, British youth are not yet directing their resentment at older generations.[68]

However such analyses ignore the straightforward clash not only of interests but also of perception between an older generation which still expects the welfare state to offer protection from the cradle to the grave and younger generations who are fast losing confidence that there will be anything left for them. People aged between 15-24 are significantly less likely than older groups to say that pensions are too low and should be raised regardless of the consequences for taxes and contributions.[69] And our *Socioconsult* analysis shows that whereas 43.2 per cent of 18-34 year old women see pensions as primarily national government's responsibility this compares to 55 per cent of 35-54 year olds.

It is quite possible to envisage a polarisation of demands. The worst excesses of generational politics US style will probably be avoided. But the once assumed generational contract is fraying at the edges – and in ways that are scarcely addressed by such halfhearted policy proposals as further cuts in inheritance tax.[70]

The result is an uneasy stalemate. If the contract is to be shored up, we need to think imaginatively not just about the implicit deals that are struck between generations, but also about the deals struck between a government and political system on the one hand, and young people on the other.

Reconnecting democracy

The first step is to reconnect politics: to make it more accessible and more meaningful so as to restore trust. The potentially explosive alienation we have uncovered requires a different approach to politics – new styles of leadership, new languages, and new mechanisms. We know that young people want more honest and open styles of leadership; ones that fit their attachment to authenticity. We know that the problem of trust can only be addressed by governments delivering on their promises. But what could be done in terms of policy to re-engage commitment?

Mechanisms for greater involvement

A more educated and demanding electorate expects to be consulted far more than in the past. As Demos has outlined elsewhere there is a range of new tools for involvement now available, including referendums, voter juries, targeted consultations, and uses of new technologies.[71]

Our evidence from the *Socioconsult* survey shows that almost 70 per cent of people aged between 18-34 would be keen to use TVs, telephones or computers for voting at elections. Even now Parliamentary debates and other Parliamentary business could be placed on the Internet to encourage open government and informed debate.

But the best way to make voting and participation easier would be to hold both local and national elections over a weekend or a whole week,[72] and to relocate polling stations.[73] Texas has shown how longer voting periods encourage many more people – particularly first-time voters and minorities – to vote.[74]

Britain needs to think far more imaginatively about relocating polling stations to DSS offices, training centres, sports clubs, university campuses or multiplex cinemas. Polling cards could include a map showing the location of polling stations.[75]

All of these initiatives could be preludes to the use of smart cards to transform voting patterns still further by making it possible for voters to vote at any time of the day or night, just as people today use cards to gain access to money.

One of the problems of disconnection is that it breeds
ignorance. Whilst it would be wrong to expect too much
of education, Britain has a particularly baleful record so
far as civic and political education is concerned. Whilst
the 1988 Education Reform Act requires schools to teach
pupils about the experiences and responsibilities of
adult life through Personal and Social Education, it does
not prescribe what should be taught. Nor is there any
central responsibility for civic and political education.

Other countries take these things much more
seriously. In Australia, Electoral Education Centres teach
school pupils about elections and voting[76] (and are being
backed up by a $25 million civic education programme
in schools).[77] In Canada, 'Elections Canada' has developed
an education initiative targeted not only at schools but
also at adults. Election simulation kits have proven the
most popular method of teaching the electoral process
and plans are being developed to put interactive
computer games and electronic information in kiosks in
airports and shopping centres.[78]

A recent survey in Britain found that 65 per cent of
respondents felt that they knew 'just a little' or 'hardly
anything' about the way Parliament works, and 69 per
cent felt the same about the British constitution.[79] The
same survey found that awareness about the workings of
Parliament, the constitution and citizens rights had
actually worsened since 1991. Given their extensive
coverage of Westminster politics this is a fairly damning
indictment of the popular press and the evening news.
We have also been struck in our qualitative research by
the level of ignorance about registration and voting
amongst young people.[80] Yet the experience of Australia
confirms that it is often ignorance which breeds apathy
and alienation rather than vice versa.[81]

We would recommend that election simulation kits,
similar to those being developed in Canada, should be
available in easily accessible places. There should also be
a legal obligation on schools to teach civic education as

115

part of personal and social education, along with fully simulated elections to coincide with local and national elections so that today's schoolchildren grow up with a basic knowledge of how to vote.[82] These initiatives could be coordinated by an independent Election Commission, established on a similar basis to those operating in Canada and Australia.[83]

Easing registration

Registration has become a particularly live issue in the 1990s. Millions of young people have slipped off the register because of the poll tax, homelessness, and mobility – at the time of the last census in 1991, 21 per cent of 21-24 year olds were not registered. Yet the government spends only 1.2p per elector on promoting registration.[84] In Australia[85] by contrast, the fact that 35.5 per cent of 18-19 year olds have never been enrolled has set off a wave of activity around registration and civic education.[86] The Electoral Commission is currently finalising a youth enrolment programme including a Student Youth Enrolment campaign and general advertising about enrolment to improve registration rates.[87]

In Britain the Home Office has begun to undertake some limited promotion of registration by advertising in newspapers and individual local authorities like Brighton have taken initiatives. But far more could be done, using the BBC and commercial media, advertising campaigns and more targeted approaches for people becoming 18. Registration packs should also be available in easily accessible places: shopping centres; workplaces and public libraries as well as schools, technical colleges and higher education institutions.

But it is hard not to escape the conclusion that the whole registration system needs to be modernised. A third of the population are estimated to have moved during the cycle of the register,[88] and young people are the most mobile group. A saner approach – and one which is far more feasible in an age of computers – would be to have a rolling register which would allow people to add their names to the register up to a week prior to election day.

Britain also needs to find ways of making registration more or less automatic. We should copy innovative schemes in the US, like the 'Motor Voter' law which links registration to driving licenses, and which is forecast to add as many as 20 million to the electoral rolls by 1996.[89] We would also recommend encouraging banks to link bank account opening for 18 year olds to registration, and the DSS to do the same for 18 year olds without jobs.

Other countries have raised the profile of registration and elections in other ways. The *Rock the Vote* campaign launched in America prior to the last Presidential election helped to ensure that first time voters played an important role in Clinton's victory[90] and it has also been given much of the credit for the rise in the percentage of under-25s who voted.[91] Since then, Youth Vote 94 has brought together a coalition of groups committed to improving voter registration and participation among 18-24 year olds, whilst 'Lead or Leave' has launched a 'Register Once' campaign calling for registration to be allowed on University campuses.[92] Although there are negative aspects to the politicisation of generational issues in the USA, one of its virtues is that, unlike in Britain, there are many more Generation X politicians standing for election.[93]

In the UK it has been left to the voluntary sector to highlight the importance of registering to vote. Both the British Youth Council and Activ88, the youth wing of Charter 88 have recently committed to an active peer-led registration campaign to encourage young people to register. Modelled on *Rock the Vote* it aims to recruit rock role models to enthuse young people, advertising in cinemas as well as recruiting at sites where young people are present. Given the cultural influence of popular music on today's youth – 41 per cent of 15-24 year olds visit a nightclub or disco once a month[94] – other ventures to encourage young people to register and vote such as that proposed by the Ministry of Sound, a global nightclub venue, are also likely to resonate with young people's experiences and appeal to them in a style they understand.

There are some problems with such initiatives: in the US, it turned out that some of the *Rock the Vote* musicians didn't themselves vote, which then led to further scepticism.[95] But all of them nevertheless raise awareness that if young people fail to engage with the political system they are likely to suffer from its decisions.

A framework of citizens' rights and responsibilities: the case for required voting

In order to reverse people's alienation from politics, there now needs to be a much greater commitment to open government, to freedom of information and more clearly set out rights, including in our view the right of 16 year olds to vote – on the principle that there should be no taxation without representation.[96] Our own analysis shows that 95 per cent of people aged between 18-34 think that they have a right to be informed about everything the Government does that might affect them. The recent MORI State of the Nation poll also found that 18-34 year olds are only marginally less rights conscious than older generations.[97]

However a framework of rights is only one element. There must also be a new emphasis upon individual political responsibility – in particular the responsibility of the individual to vote, at the core of which we believe should be a shift to required voting for national elections and referendums.

Many in Britain will see required voting as anathema. They will claim that it clashes with deeply held Anglo-Saxon views of freedom, and that it is unnecessary when turnout is still over 70 per cent for general elections. However, in our view the requirement to spend a few minutes voting every few years is a far lesser evil than the prospect of disconnecting a substantial slice of the population from politics and power.

Although few people realise it, there already is compulsion. Non-registration is illegal, and carries a fine of up to £1,000. Required voting would only extend this principle.

For the young there are special reasons to support a shift to required voting, since it would markedly increase their political weight. But by far the strongest argument is a more general one. From the individual point of view voting is irrational – given that in the majority of seats there is no prospect of one vote making any difference. But from the collective point of view non-voting is deeply irrational, since it makes the system less responsive and less representative.

But would required voting actually work? The Australian experience shows that the principal objections are ill-founded. First introduced in 1924 for Federal elections, all elections in Australia are now compulsory.[98] In a similar political culture to Britain, the requirement to vote has socialised many young people into taking part in the political process, and the costs – often cited as a drawback – are seen as a 'non issue'.[99] About 5 per cent of votes are spoiled (largely due to ignorance about voting procedures) and about 5 per cent of the eligible population fail to vote.[100] Computerisation of the electoral register means that they are easily identified, and given time to produce a valid reason for having failed to vote. If they are unable to do so, they are fined up to $50 – far less than the fine for non-registration in Britain. So whilst coercion in a democratic system would appear to be a contradiction in terms, it does not arouse strong passions[101] or resentment amongst young people.[102] In fact Australian youth groups see it as beneficial to society whilst requiring little effort on the part of the individual.[103]

Best of all, required voting could also improve accountability. Currently in Britain the only indicators of discontent are abstentions and the number of spoilt votes. These can be interpreted as the product of ignorance as much as overt protest. A better approach would be to redesign ballot papers to include a 'none of the above' category, with a comments box. The numbers of votes for the 'none of the above' category and the comments alongside them would be published soon after an election or referendum. This would serve as a performance indicator for the political system as a whole.

The new intergenerational contract

The second set of components of a new deal concern policy. If intergenerational conflict is to be contained, the terms of new relationships need to be defined. Governments need to be able to set out a contract with young people with achievable goals on the issues that concern young voters: practical policies on jobs and homes, on the environment and on opportunities to learn. In previous chapters we have set out some of the priorities in relation to personal relationships and to jobs.

But governments also need to be able to explain the balance of spending. Young people will become legitimately resentful if public pensions payments – many of them to relatively wealthy retired people – are seen to squeeze out benefits for poor young families, lone parents and the unemployed, all groups with less political muscle but often greater need. Similarly current social security rules that have sharply worsened the position of 16-18 year olds need to be rethought. In our view 16 year olds should be treated as adults, not only in relation to votes and work, but also in relation to tax and benefits, which now contribute to postponing their transition to adulthood.

Generational auditing
At the moment public accounts give little real insight into generational issues There is now a strong case for bringing them up to date, so as to make the balance of generational spending and revenues more transparent. Laurence Kotlikoff has put the case particularly well in

his book *Generational Accounting*. He calls for a "switch from an outdated, misleading and fundamentally non-economic measure of fiscal policy, namely the budget deficit, to generational accounting – the direct description of the government's treatment of current and prospective generations over their lifetimes".[104] Its virtue, he argues, is not only that it would bring choices into the open, but also that it would lead to more rational public and governmental decisions which take account of the long-term impact of policy decisions.

The Committee for a Responsible Federal Budget has published generational audits of US government spending programmes. In our view, government in the UK should now pioneer generational audits of its own spending and taxation programmes as a way of leading to an informed and publicly accountable debate about spending priorities.

Age, savings and welfare
Governments also need to come clean about the terms of the new social contract for this generation. We have already spelled out how this is likely to mean more spending on learning and more personal finance for time off work. But politicians also need to clearly state that despite the popular demands for earlier retirement, the reality is that retirement ages need to increase. Given that we live longer, it is hard to see how we can avoid working longer. A number of other Western countries – notably Germany, Italy, Sweden and the US – have already followed this route and others, like France, are considering it. Some countries, notably Germany, France and Spain, are also restructuring the methods of paying for pensions or making qualifications more stringent.[105] For this generation the likelihood is that many will be working well into their 70s.

But how is this generation's old age to be paid for? Longer working will be part of the answer. But on its own it is unlikely to be sufficient. The tax-based pay-as-you-go approach has probably met its limits, not least because of public resistance to tax. Incentives to encourage voluntary saving and private pensions have had some success – but far from enough. Our BHPS research shows that only 54 per cent of 16-24 year olds and 54.1 per cent of 25-34 year olds are now saving from their current income. So although personal provision is in some respects in tune with the ethos of this generation and their practices, it cannot be relied on to deliver long term security. Everyone in this generation will need to save more than their parents. But many will find it difficult, partly because of more discontinuous work. In our view long-term financial security, at least for those without marketable skills and property, may depend on some form of compulsory saving to pay for retirement. In future reports we will be spelling out in more detail how this might work in ways that are sufficiently flexible to fit with public values.

A Minister of Generations?

As governments come to terms with the new intergenerational politics there are interesting lessons to be learnt from France and Germany. In May 1995 President Chirac set up a Ministry of Solidarity Between Generations to focus on youth, the family, and senior citizens. At the press conference launching the Ministry, the new Minister said that "the debts we contract today will have to be paid by our children in ten or fifteen years. It is our responsibility not to burden their future with taxes they are not responsible for."[106] Germany too has long had a Ministry of Family, Senior Citizens, Women and Youth which functions de facto as an inter-generational ministry to take into account conflicting priorities.

We do not wish to recommend a Ministry or to add further unnecessary bureaucracy to government. However a 'generations' Minister with a cross departmental brief could help appraise inter-generational equity issues and build consensus around ways to tackle them.[107]

Conclusion

The jury is still out on how the lives of this generation will compare to their parents' and grandparents', and whether the economic and social progress of this century will continue.

We certainly know that the generation born in the 1920s and 1930s had it better than any before. For them the welfare state provided a safety net. Full employment guaranteed reasonable prosperity and security. Generous occupational and state pensions guaranteed their old age. And an era of peace saved them from the need to go to war.

Much the same was true for the generation born in the 1940s and 1950s. They could take for granted (at least until recently) steadily rising real incomes, chances to travel and opportunities for self-discovery. For women new horizons were opened up – the chance to go to university, and follow careers. Those who owned houses could sit on a steadily appreciating capital asset without lifting a finger.

In many respects the pace of change has kept up for the generation born in the 1960s and 1970s. Only in the last decade have women overtaken boys in schools and universities, marched in their thousands into the professions and taken advantage of the much more equal attitudes to gender roles that have filtered throughout all classes. Most young people remain optimistic and see their lives as better than their parents.

But things are never black or white. In other respects this generation cannot take for granted much that seemed natural 20 or 30 years ago. High unemployment and labour market insecurity have become facts of life. Security for old age is guaranteed neither by the state, as the relative value of pensions declines, nor by occupational schemes; as our research shows, 40 per cent of 25-29 year olds don't believe they'll ever get what they're owed. Meanwhile, the prevalence of negative equity amongst the young has made them understandably anxious about debt.

In relationships the benefits of greater freedom have proven inseparable from the costs, as our capacity to compromise and negotiate has not improved sufficiently to compensate for the weakening of institutions like marriage.

In political terms, however, it is the potential intergenerational imbalances which could prove most destabilising. A political backlash against the drift of public spending towards the elderly is already apparent in other countries. Some are beginning to fear that their generation will be squeezed on pensions – having to fund their own pensions while also paying through taxes for the pensions and care needs of their parents.

So far the question of how different generations relate to each other has remained off the political agenda in Britain. In part this reflects just how much young people are disconnected from parties and parliament. This is why we have argued for new approaches to voting, registration and participation as vital to any restoration of intergenerational solidarity.

In the short-term young people's disengagement may reinforce the complacency of older groups. After all, if people don't vote their views don't count. But in the long-run this disconnection is not just about votes – it is also about social cohesion and people's willingness to play by the rules. Our fear is that failure to take intergenerational politics seriously could threaten a much wider social unravelling, affecting everything from crime to everyday behaviour. What we have described as the 'underwolves' – the underdogs who are now biting back – have the capacity to ruin pretty much everyone's quality of life.

But our broader argument concerns the balance between freedom and commitment. For Britain as for other societies this is new territory. No previous generation has been brought up with such an inheritance of freedoms, such opportunities and such a range of often daunting choices. For no previous generation has tradition been such an unhelpful guide. The challenge for those we have called Freedom's Children is therefore a difficult one. No-one wants to lose hardwon freedoms. There really is no turning back to the family structures and hierarchies of the past.

But few will thrive in a world without any clear commitments.That is why we have argued for a new balance, whether in the rules governing parents and cohabitees, and fathers and mothers, or in the rules governing the relationships between employers and employees.

For policy-makers the challenge is to avoid facile solutions and devise workable frameworks of commitment that fit modern values. It goes without saying that this won't be easy. It requires us to think as much about culture as the more familiar paraphernalia of policies and programmes. But the price of failure could be so high, whether in terms of relationship breakdown, unemployment or even chronic violence. This is a challenge we can no longer afford to ignore.

Notes

The fracturing of British values

1. See Inglehart, R., 1971 'The Silent Revolution in Europe: Intergenerational change in post-industrial societies' *American Political Science Review* 65:991-1017, Inglehart, R., 1977 *The silent revolution: Changing values and political styles among Western publics,* Princeton and Inglehart R., 1990, *Culture Shift in Advanced Industrial Society*, Princeton. In this book Inglehart goes further and tries to explain this shift to post material values as part of an inter-generational shift in values.

2.Inglehart, R., 1990; 1

3. Halpern, D., 1995, 'Values, Morals and Modernity: The values, constraints and norms of European youth', in Rutter, M. and Smith, J., eds. 1995, *Psychosocial Disorders in Young People: Time trends and their causes*, John Wiley and Sons; 381.

4. 'NetFacts', 1994, Liberation technology, *Demos Quarterly* Issue 4, Demos.

5. Wilkinson, H.,1994, *No Turning Back: generations and the genderquake,* Demos. This report presented data of value shifts in Britain over a period of twenty years.

6. *The Moral Values of Young People*, MORI poll amongst 1,200 young people aged 15-35 conducted on 18-22 August 1994. Wroe, M., 1994, 'Young Adrift in Moral Maze', *The Observer,* 9 October.

7. See Modood, T., Beishon, S., and Virdee, S., 1994, *Changing Ethnic Identities*, Policy Studies Institute, London. This trend was confirmed by phase one of Demos' qualitative research, the details of which can be found in the appendix to this report.

8. See Ahrendt, D. and Young, K., 1994, 'Authoritarianism Updated' in *British Social Attitudes, the 11th report* , Dartmouth Publishing; 80. Authoritarians are also more likely to be Conservative, to have no qualifications, to be Social Classes V and IV and to be religious. See also Heath, A. and McMahon, D., 1991, in *British Social Attitudes, the 8th report*, Dartmouth Publishing for the relationship between an 'authoritarian' mindset and allegiances to 'moral traditionalism' which are also closely correlated with age.

9. Halpern, D., 1995; 347

10. See Wilkinson, H.,1994; 12-16.

11. See *Youth Lifestyles*, Mintel, 1995 24 March.

12. Parallel studies conducted over a number of years in France Germany and North America have demonstrated that this value, 'crude hedonism', has been giving way to 'discerning' hedonism, a value in the social/modern quartile of the map which is related to the valuing (savouring) of time. *Socioconsult International*, Paris

13. Halpern, D., 1995; 375-77

Working life – balancing opportunity and security

1. Gregg, P., and Wadsworth, J., 1995, 'A Short History of Labour Turnover, Job Tenure and Job Security', 1973-93, *Oxford Review of Economic Policy*, Volume 11.

2. Buck, N., Gershuny, J., Rose, D., Scott, J., 1994, *Changing Households: The British Household Panel Survey 1990 - 1992*, ERSC Research Centre On Micro-Social Change.

3. Mulgan, G., and Wilkinson, H., 1995, `Well-being and Time', The time squeeze, *Demos Quarterly* Issue 5, Demos.

4. Bridges, W., 1995, *Job Shift: How to Prosper in a World Without Jobs*, Allen and Unwin.

5. Moss Kanter, R., 1994, Employability and Job Security in the 21st Century, The end of unemployment, *Demos Quarterly* Issue 2, Demos.

6. Henley Centre for Forecasting, 1994, *Planning for Social Change*, Volume 1: Structural Trends; 21-22, 7.

7. *Long-term Employment Strategies*, 1995 (forthcoming), Institute of Management/Manpower.

8. Henley Centre for Forecasting, 1994, Volume 2; Analysis and Implications;8.

9. *Social Trends 25*, 1995, CSO; 74. Trade union membership in the United

Kingdom fell by nearly 6 per cent in 1992, its sharpest fall since 1981. It now stands at 36 per cent compared to the rates of over 50 per cent experienced in the 1970s and union membership has now reached its lowest level since 1946.

10. The time squeeze, *Demos Quarterly* Issue 5, 1995.

11. Burgess S., and Rees, H., 1994; 9, 28. The concept of 'job-shopping' has been applied to young people due to higher rates of job turnover amongst this group than older generations. However, those jobs available to young people are more insecure than in the past. Gregg and Wadsworth, 1995; 4 point out that it is amongst these younger workers that most of the absolute rise in turnover has occurred.

12. Gregg, P., and Wadsworth, J., 1995; 1.

13. This is according to our figures from the BHPS. Younger men feel that their father's generation had 'the better deal' with respect of jobs and job security. This has been a major strand of discussions in the Young Men Qualitative Research project, the details of which are provided in the end of this report

14. MERIC, 1994, *GenX:Euro, Abort, Retry, Ignore?* McCann-Erickson Research and Information Consultancy. See also Samms, C., 1995, *Global Generation X: Their Values and Attitudes*, Working Paper 8, Demos.

15. See for example, Sampson, A., 1995, Chapter Fifteen, 'Daddy's Run Away', *Company Man: The Rise and Fall of Corporate Life*, Harper Collins; 220-229.

16. Employment Department figures for 1994/5 estimated that 45 per cent of the labour market was constituted of women. See: *Women and Employment Factsheet*, 1995. Figures used by the Economist suggest that the proportion may be marginally higher, at 49.5 per cent. See: The Economist, 1995, *Pocket Britain in Figures*, Penguin; 83.

17. Joshi, H., and Paci, P., 1995, *Wage Differentials Between Men and Women*, Department of Employment; 34. This research on the gender pay gap finds that since 1978 the impact of the education and training deficit on women's wages, known amongst analysts as the 'attribute gap', has decreased from 9 per cent to just 0.4 per cent by 1991. Amongst the younger age range (16-24 years) the attribute gap has almost completely closed, as girls increasingly outperform boys at school.

18. Harkness, S., and Machin, S., 1995 forthcoming, *Changes in Women's Wages in Britain: What has Happened to the Female/Male Wage Differential Since the Mid 1970's?*, Centre for Economic Performance, London School of Economics. Their report finds a significant closing of the gender gap amongst younger women relative to women of the same age twenty years ago. For example, the gap has closed from 81.8 per cent in 1975-1977 to 91.8 in 1990-92 for women with degrees aged between 16-24 and from 81.2 per cent to 88.6 per cent for women with A levels.

19. See for example Coyle, A., 1995, *Learning from Experience: The Equal Opportunities Challenge for the 1990s* , Working Paper 5, Demos.

20. Rubery, J., and Fagan, C., 1994, 'Occupational Segregation: Plus ca Change....?', in Lindley, R., ed, 1994, *Labour Market Structures and Prospects for Women*, Research Series, EOC. Also see the TUC 1994 report, *Women in the Labour Market – Analysis of What Has Happened to Women's Employment and Education and Training Prospects in the 1990s.*

21. Labour Force Survey figures in *Women and Employment Factsheet* 1995. Figures cited for Winter 1994/95 and Autumn 1995 respectively.

22. Mouriki, A., 1994, *Flexible Working: Towards Further Degradation of Work, or Escaping from Stereotypes*, Warwick Paper in Industrial Relations.

23. Rubery, J., and Fagan, C., 1994. See also Joshi, H., and Hinde, P.R.A., 1993, Employment After Childbearing in Post War Britain: Cohort-Study Evidence on Contrasts within and across Generations, *European Sociological Review*, Volume 9, No 3, Dec 1993, Oxford University Press. This paper provides evidence of continuing job downgrading and provides a cautionary note on interpreting increased employment as an improvement in female status.

24. Joshi, H., and Paci, P., 1995. See also: Dex, S., Lissenburgh, S., and Taylor, M., 1994. *Women and Low Pay: Identifying the Issues*, Discussion Series, EOC. See also: Harkness, S., and Machin, S., 1995 (forthcoming). For young women (16-24) with four O levels or less the pay gap has hardly closed at all.

25. For example, see: Barclay, Sir P., 1995, *Joseph Rowntree Foundation Inquiry into Income and Wealth*, Volume 1, Joseph Rowntree Foundation and Hills, J., 1995, *Joseph Rowntree Foundation Inquiry into Income and Wealth*, Volume 2, Joseph Rowntree Foundation.

26. *Social Focus on Women*, CSO; 8.

27. Harkness S., Machin, S., and Waldfogel, J., 1995, *Evaluating the Pin Money Hypothesis: The Relationship Between Women's Labour Market Activity, Family Income and Poverty in Britain*, Discussion Paper No. WSP/108, Welfare State Programme, Centre for Economic Performance, LSE; 16. This report considers the importance of women's earnings to the maintenance of household, disclaiming the assertion that women who work are earning `pin money'. They argue that in the 1990s, the presence of a male breadwinner within a household cannot be taken for granted, and that women's earnings have grown in importance dramatically over recent years. They partly attribute this to low wages and poverty.

28. *Social Trends 25*, 1995, HMSO, 70

29. According to our analysis of Wave 1 of BHPS, the figures are: 49.2 per cent for over 56 year olds to just 36.5 per cent, barely a third of 16-24 year old men.

30. Rubery J., and Fagan, C., 1994.

31. See Joshi, H., 1990, 'The Cash Opportunity Costs of Childbearing: An Approach To Estimation Using British Data', *Population Studies*, 44, 1990; 41-60, for a detailed analysis of these opportunity costs on a range of criteria and Joshi, H., and Paci, P., 1995; 34.

32. Waldfogel, J., 1993, *Women Working for Less: A Longitudinal Analysis of the Family Gap*, Discussion Paper No. WSP/93, Welfare State Programme, Centre for Economic Performance, LSE: 16.

33. Joshi, H., and Paci, P., 1995

34. Harkness, S., and Machin, S., 1995 (forthcoming).

35. This has been confirmed by Demos' qualitative research (see appendix).

36. Jowell, R., Curtice, J., Brook L., and Ahrendt, D., 1994; 44. This trend has also been observed in the qualitative research conducted by Demos as part of this project.

37 Cannon, D., 1995, *Generation X and the New Work Ethic*, Working Paper 1, Demos.

38. Similar findings are also reported in a 1990 European Values Survey cited in Halpern, D., 1995; 369.

39. 1990 European Values Survey cited in Halpern, D., 1995; 368.

40. Harding, S., 1992, *Changing Expectations and Opinions of Employees: Results from Recent Research*, Paper prepared for conference 'Increased Motivation, Performance and Productivity', 24-25 March 1992, London.

41. Demos has conducted a series of casestudies in three different sectors of the economy. See Wilkinson, H., 1995 *Equality and Diversity in a Time of Change: a case study of regional broadcasting*, Working Paper 10, Demos, Wilkinson, H., and Bentley, T., 1995, *Equality and Diversity: a casestudy of young professionals*, Working Paper 11, Demos, Wilkinson, H., 1995, *Through the Eyes of Shop Floor Workers: equal opportunities in manufacturing*, Working Paper 12, Demos.

42. See Wilkinson, H and Bentley, T., 1995, Working Paper 11. See also

Halpern, 1995; 369. He argues that people are becoming more concerned about pay and promotion, and less concerned about a job's usefulness to society.

43. The class differences seemed most acute between ABC1 and C2DE women: the former are more likely to see work as a source of meaning at 51 per cent where as C2DE women are considerably less likely to see their work as a source of meaning. We also observed this trend in our focus groups.

44. There is little difference between women across the class range. Amongst men there is a different pattern. C2DE men rely on work as a source of meaning (55 per cent) more extensively than ABC1 men (45 per cent). We also analysed the data to take account of lifestage. Women in relationships with children were more likely to demand less from their work than young single women and women in relationships without children. There was a similar pattern with single parent women.

45. This has been evident in our qualitative research and we have subsequently been able to quantify this trend through *Socioconsult*.

46. This has been confirmed in our qualitative research. See for example, Wilkinson, H., 1995, Working Paper 12.

47. Robinson, P., 1995, *Qualifications and the labour market: do the national education and training targets make sense?*, WP No. 736 Centre for Economic Performance, No.736, London School of Economics.

48. For more information on this see the appendix for details of the qualitative research and the casestudies.

49. Note that the really big shift is from the 56+ to the next age group of men and women below. Thereafter we see a continuation and acceleration of a trend.

50. These findings have also been confirmed by our latest focus groups as part of the research project on young men and also by our work with shop floor workers in a manufacturing firm. See Wilkinson, H., 1995, Working Paper 12.

51. We controlled for class differences. The gender trend held up. Nor did we find strong class effects. In general ABC1s were coping better than C2DEs

52. In our qualitative research concern was expressed about the difficulties of achieving this in the current jobs climate

53. See for example Wilkinson, H., 1995, Working Paper 12.

54. See Cannon, D., 1994, for his description of Generation X's perceptions of Winner and Loser organisations. This trend has also been observed in our qualitative research, especially inside companies. See Wilkinson, H., 1995, Working Paper 10 and 12, and Wilkinson, H., and Bentley, T., 1995, Working Paper 11.

55. See Winkfield, N., 1995, 'Bad Timing: Attitudes to the New World of Work', The time squeeze, *Demos Quarterly* Issue 5, Demos, for more of an explanation of this social trend. The Henley Centre for Forecasting, 1994, also concludes that ..."consumers, faced with a more complex and uncertain world are turning back to those familiar relationships which they trust most." Volume 2; 35.

56. The time squeeze, 1995, *Demos Quarterly* Issue No 5, Demos

57. This has been a consistent theme throughout our qualitative research. It is more likely to be expressed and articulated by higher educated employees than less educated employees.

58. The base of single parent males is small and so these findings should be treated with some caution.

59. This has been evident throughout our extensive qualitative research. For more detail refer to the appendix. See also Cannon, D., 1994.

60. Herriot, P., and Pemberton, C., 1995, *New Deals: The Revolution in Managerial Careers*, John Wiley and Sons.

61. Henley Centre for Forecasting, 1994, Volume 2; 33.

62. See Wilkinson, H., 1995, Working Papers 10 and 12, and also Wilkinson, H., and Bentley, T., 1995, Working Paper 11.

63. In their lack of faith, this generation of men seem no different to the 35-55 age range of men - 34 per cent of whom are worried. Younger women however seem considerably less likely than older women to be worried about their pension: 35 per cent of the 35-55 year old women are concerned compared to 22 per cent of 18-34 year old women.

64. See Cannon, D., 1994 Working Paper 1, and Samms, C., Working Paper 8, 1995.

65. Bridges, W., 1994. This book details various examples where this has been the case in American companies.

66. For a detailed analysis of the costs of insecurity and stress on people's working lives and also the impact on family life see: The time squeeze, 1995, *Demos Quarterly* Issue 5. It includes the most up to date facts and statistics on attitudes to work. An inquiry into the daycare needs of shiftworkers found that 42 per cent of parents reported problems with arranging childcare, even on uniform shifts, Kozak, M., 1994, *Not Just Nine to Five - A Survey of Shift Workers' Childcare Needs*, Daycare

Trust; 5.

67. See Fukuyama, F., 1995, *Trust: The Social Virtues and Creation of Prosperity*, Free Press, New York and Hamish Hamilton, London. For more information on the impact of flexible labour markets upon the provision of training, see: CBI, 1994, *Flexible Labour Markets: Who Pays for Training?*, Confederation of British Industry.

68. See *Tomorrow's Company: The Role of Business in a Changing World*, 1994, Interim Report, RSA Inquiry; 15-16. Thorn EMI Hayes Middlesex factory had to reduce its workforce from 700 to 150. It succeeded in doing this by compensating those made redundant with training certification. At Chaparral Steel in the USA, employees are encouraged to make suggestions, even where these will lead to the disappearance of their own jobs, protected by a guarantee that the company will find them alternative employment. Fisher, S., 'Cutting Costs or Rebuilding Business?', *European Management Journal* , Volume 11, No 1; 76.

69. Guzzo, R.A., Nelson, G.L., and Noonan, K.A., 1992, 'Commitment and Employer Involvement in Employees' Nonwork Lives', in Zadeck, S., ed, 1992, *Work, Families and Organisations*, Jossey Bass, San Francisco. This report lists a variety of ways in which employee commitment can be re-engaged.

70. See for example the detailed qualitative research report amongst representative samples of the UK population and also the casestudies of three different sectors of the economy.

71. In this instance the base includes those in work and those out of work and the 12 month period is from the point at which the interview was conducted. These figures are from Demos' analysis of the BHPS, Wave 3 (see appendix)

72. Gallie D., and White, M., 1993, *Employee Commitment and the Skills Revolution*, Policy Studies Institute.

73. See for example Wilkinson, H., 1995, Working Paper 12. Here it is quite clear that there is no business case for investing in education and training with any of these unskilled or relatively skilled workers.

74. 'Skilless Youth costs Britain Millions', BTEC, 14 August 1995, press release based on findings of an unpublished survey.

75. Heilman M.E., 1994, 'Affirmative Action: Some Unintended Consequences for Working Women', *Research in Organizational Behaviour*, 16; 125-169, 164.

76. Kandola, R., and Fullerton, J., 1994, *Managing the Mosaic: Diversity in Action* Chapter 5, 'Diversity Initiatives'; 72.

77. Kandola, R., and Fullerton, J., 1994, Chapter 9 gives a detailed account of this question. Their analysis is also very similar to the analysis that we have reached through our discussions with young men and women in various organisations, some where there are targets, others where there are not.

78. See Coe, T., 1992, *The Key to the Men's Club,* Institute of Management; 17-22, which reported that only 25 per cent of women and 15 per cent of men believed that their organisation should use quotas.

79. Demos has conducted three casestudies in three different sectors of the economy. One organisation has targets and uses a positive action approach whilst the other two do not. In each case we find that women are resistant to any form of 'special' and targeted schemes. See for example, Wilkinson, H., 1995, Working Papers 10, and 12, or Wilkinson, H., and Bentley, T., 1995, Working Paper, 11.

80. Coyle, A, 1995, Working Paper 5. Drawing on her extensive work in five sectors of the economy for the EOC. Angela Coyle argues that some companies have managed to look as if they have met their targets without any objective improvement in women's promotion opportunities as companies have downsized. See also, Kandola, R., and Fullerton, J., 1994; 149.

81. The sample of professional women with children is small. As a result the figure for professional women should be treated with some caution.

82. See Bond, J., 1992, 'The Impact of Childbearing on Employment', in Freidman, D.E., Gallinsky, E., and Ploden, V., 1992, *Parental Leave and Productivity*, Current Research, Families and Work Institute. Also, Staines, G., L., and Galinsky, E., 1992, 'Parental Leave and Productivity: The Supervisors's View', in Freidman, D.E., Galinsky, E., and Plowden, V., Eds, 1992, *Parental Leave and Productivity*, Current Research, Families and Work Institute.

83. Staines, G.L. and Galinsky, E., 1993; 84.

84. New Ways to Work, 1993, *Change at the Top: Working Flexibly at Senior and Managerial Levels in Organisations*, New Ways to Work; 20.

85. Cooper, C. and Lewis, S., 1995, *Beyond family friendly organisations*, Working Paper 2. This has also been reinforced by Demos' own casestudies in particular companies. See also the large body of evidence amassed in The time squeeze, 1995, *Demos Quarterly* Issue 5.

86. See Mulgan, G., and Wilkinson, H., 1995, *Demos Quarterly* Issue 5 for more details on Work/Life programmes.

87. The European Commission's Families and Work Network awarded prizes to a range of organisations across Europe in June 1995.

88. For more on this see: Cooper, C., and Lewis, S., 1995, Working Paper 2.

89. Mulgan, G., and Wilkinson, H., 1995, *Demos Quarterly* Issue 5.

90. These would be helped if governments allowed deferred salary to be assigned to a trust to finance time off, so that pay accumulates tax free until it is drawn down. In such cases employers could also be permitted national insurance rebates on that portion of income which is being paid into that trust. Such 'time banks' already exist in Ontario and could be linked into personal and occupational pension schemes.

91. This has been confirmed in our focus groups with unemployed young men.

92. Wadsworth, J. and Gregg, P., 1995.

93. According to MERIC, 1994, *Gen X: Euro, Abort, Retry, Ignore?* McCann Erickson Research and Information Consultancy.

94. Wadsworth, J., and Gregg, P., 1995, 6

95. Collected from Demos' Young Men project.

96. Gosling, A., Machin, S., and Meghir, C., 1994, 'What has happened to men's wages since the mid-1960s', *Fiscal Studies.*

97. Briscoe, I., 1995, *In Whose Service?*, Arguments 2, Demos.

98. See: *Foyers for young people: evaluation of a pilot initiative,* 1995, Centre for Housing Policy, University of York.

99. Briscoe, I., 1995, 'Time Rights in the 1990s: An International Survey', *Demos Quarterly* Issue 5; 37.

100. Walker, A., 1993, 'Whither the Social Contract? Intergenerational Solidarity in Income and Employment', in Hobman, D., 1993, *Uniting Generations: Studies in Conflict and Cooperation*, Age Concern.

101. For further information on community service for old people in America see: Freedman, M., 1994. *Seniors in National and Community Service: A Report prepared for The Commonwealth Fund's Americans Over 55 At Work Program*, Public Private Ventures.

102. *Jobs, Education and Training (JET) Facts Sheets*, Family Programs Division, Canberra Department of Social Security, 1993.

Renegotiating relationships and parenting

1. Randall, C., and Hibbs, J., 1995, Marriages at lowest level for 50 years, *The Daily Telegraph*, 23 August.

2. The Economist, 1994, *Pocket Britain in Figures*, Penguin, London; 180 and Utting, D., 1995, *Family and Parenthood: Supporting Families, Preventing Breakdown*, Joseph Rowntree Foundation.

3. *Something to Celebrate: Valuing Families in Church and Society*, Working Party report, Church of England's Board for Social Responsibility, 1995; 36.

4. Mattison, K., McAllister, F., and Roberts, K., 1994, *Divorce Today*, Factsheet 4, One Plus One.

5. Mattison, K., et al, 1994, *Marriage Today*, Factsheet 1, One Plus One.

6. Gillis, J.R., 1985, *For Better For Worse: British Marriages 1600 to the Present*, Oxford University Press, Oxford.

7. Mattison, K., 1994, *Marriage Today*, Factsheet 1, One Plus One.While the marriage rate per 1,000 has halved, the absolute number of marriages has fallen by a quarter between 1971 and 1992 according to *Social Focus on Women*, 1995; 14. The fastest decline has been in the number of first time marriages. These fell by 4 per cent between 1983 and 1993, whilst the number of remarriages rose by 1 per cent during the same period according to figures in *Population Trends* 79, 1995.

8. Laurance, J., 1995, Divorces Rise and fewer get married, *The Times*, 23 August citing latest figures from the OPCS.

9. Bellos, A., 1995, Slump Blamed for record divorces, *The Guardian*, 23 August & Laurance, J., Divorces Rise and fewer get married, *The Times*, 23 August citing figures from the OPCS.

10. Mattison, K., et al, 1994, *Marriage Today*, Factsheet 1 , One Plus One, and also *Social Focus on Women*, CSO, 1995; 14.

11. Preston, M.,'Cover for Wedding Mishaps', *The Times*, 18 March 1995.

12. McRae, S.,1993, *Cohabiting Mothers: Changing Marriage and Motherhood?*, Policy Studies Institute; 46. Those most deterred by the costs of a big white wedding were the youngest of the long-term cohabiting mothers and were the least likely to hold qualifications or to be in paid work; 48.

13. Mattison, K., et al, 1994, *Marriage Today*, Factsheet 1 , One Plus One.

14. Furbisher, J., and Rayment, J., 1992, 'Recession Takes a toll on love and marriage', *Sunday Times*, 23 August.

15. Mansfield, P., 1985, *Young People and Marriage*, Scottish Marriage Guidance Council, Edinburgh.

16. McRae, S., 1993, 46.

17. Mattison, K., et al, 1994, *Divorce Today*, Factsheet 4, One Plus One

18. Ermisch, J., 1993, 'Familia Oeconomica: A Survey of the Economics of the Family', *Scottish Journal of Political Economy*, Volume 40, No 4; 357-

358.

19. Dormor, D.J., 1992, *The Relationship Revolution: Cohabitation, Marriage and Divorce in Contemporary Europe*, One Plus One; 20.

20. Social and Community Planning Research, 1992, *British Social Attitudes: cumulative sourcebook: the first six surveys*, Gower; N.1 - 14. In 1990 the European Values Survey also found that mutual respect, appreciation and faithfulness, understanding, tolerance and a happy sexual relationship were deemed the four most successful elements of a happy marriage. More practical factors such as good housing, an adequate income, and living apart from the in-laws, were much lower down the list, cited in Dormor, D.J., 1992; 20.

21. Lewis, J., Clark, D., and Morgan, D, 1992, *Whom God Hath Joined Together*, Routledge, London. This book gives a detailed analysis of the defining characteristics of marriage as an institution to marriage as a relationship.

22. Dormor, D.J.,; 20. Other argue that unrealistic expectations have been set for modern egalitarian marriages in which people have unrealistic expectations and expect to marry both a lover and a best friend according to: Reibstein, J., *Marriages: Monogamy and Affairs* cited by Weale, S., 'Common Foible, Usual Criticism,, 1995, *The Guardian,* 23 March

23. Weale, S, 1995, 'Common Foible, Usual Criticism', *The Guardian*, 23 March. This article cites research in Lawson, A., *Adultery, Analysis and Betrayal* and from *British Social Attitudes.*

24. Weale, S., 1995, 'Common Foible, Usual Criticism', *The Guardian*, 23 March, citing Judy Corlyn, former research officer at the London School of Economics, now at the National Children's Bureau.

25. Dormor, D.J.,; 26-27.

26. Weldon, F., 1995, 'Is this all New Woman can Want from New Marriage?', *The Evening Standard*, 12 May 1995 citing paper presented by Carol Smart from Leeds University, Department of Sociology. 'Changing attitudes towards adultery', One Plus One conference, 11 May 1995.

27. Buck, N., and Scott, J., 1994, 'Household and Family Change', in Buck, N., Gershuny, J., Rose, D., and Scott, J., eds, *Changing Households: The British Household Panels Survey* 1990-92 , ESRC Research Centre on Micro-Social Change; 62.

28. *Social Focus on Women*, 1995, CSO; 13.

29. Dormor, D.J., 1992; 8.

30. Ermisch, J., 1995, *Pre-Marital Cohabitation, Childbearing and the Creation*

of One Parent Families, Working Paper 95-17, ESRC Research Centre on Micro-Social Change; 9 & 3-4.

31. Mattison, K., et al, 1994, *Cohabitation*, Factsheet 3, One Plus One.

32. Ermisch, J., 1995; 12.

33. Buck, N., and Scott, J., 1994, 'Household and Family Change', Buck, N., et al, eds, 1994; 62.

34. *Social Focus on Women*, 1995;14.

35. McRae, S., 1993; 46.

36. This has been confirmed in phase one of Demos' qualitative research. See appendix for further details.

37. McRae, S., 1993; 51.

38. Of under 35 year olds sampled in 1989 only 18 per cent would advise a young man or woman to marry without living together first. Of those cohabiting, 68 per cent would advise a young person to cohabit and then marry whilst 20 per cent of cohabitees would advise living with someone without marrying. British Social Attitudes, 1989 cited in: Kiernan, K.E., and Estaugh, V., 1993, *Cohabitation: Extra-marital Childbearing and Social Policy*, Occasional Paper 17, Family Policy Studies Centre; 7.

39. Wellings, K., Field, J., Johnson, A.M. and Wadsworth, J., 1994, *Sexual Behaviour in Britain: The National Survey of Sexual Attitudes and Lifestyles*, Penguin; 116.

40. McRae, S., 1993, 51-52

41. Buck, N., and Scott, J., 1994, 'Household and Family Change', in Buck, N, et al, eds, 1994; 61.

42. Ermisch, J., 1995; 12.

43. Mattison, K., et al, 1994, *Divorce Today*, Factsheet 4, One Plus One.

44. *Social Trends 25*, 1995; 39.

45. Mills, E., 1994, '20th Century Woman', Life, *The Observer*, 6 November, and also *Social Trends 25*, 1995.

46. Babb, P., 1995, 'Fertility of the Over Forties', *Population Trends*, OPCS.

47. *Social Focus on Women*, 1995; 15.

48. Lightfoot, L., and Wavell, S., 1995, 'Mum's Not The Word', *The Sunday Times*, 16 April, citing Bartlett, J., *Will You Be Mother? Women Who Choose To Say No*.

49. *Social Focus on Women*, 1995; 16.

50. This prediction was made in the Family Policy Studies Centre Bulletin, April 1995 and was reported in several newspapers including: *The Guardian*, 1995, 'Work blamed as one in 5 women expected not to bear children', 10 April and Grant, L., 1995 No Kids on the Block, *The*

Guardian, 11 April, and Timmins, N., 1995, 'One in Five Women to Remain Childless', *The Independent*, 10 April.

51. *Social Trends 25*, HMSO, 1995; 42. Figures also cited in: Working Party Report, 1995, Church of England's Board for Social Responsibility; 36. The overall trend of births outside of marriage is mentioned in: *How to Make A Family Covenant: Child Welcoming Ceremonies*, 1994, The Family Covenant Association; 2. Kiernan, K., and Estaugh, V., 1993; 24, also argue that their analysis shows that since the 1980's children are being increasingly born to never married women.

52. Ermisch, J., 1995; 11.

53. *British Social Attitudes 1989* cited in Kiernan, K., and Estaugh, V., 1993; 7-8, which suggests that younger people, those currently cohabiting and former cohabitants, are more permissive about childbearing outside marriage than older people, the married and those who marry directly.

54. Mattison, K., et al, 1994, *Impact of Divorce*, Factsheet 5, One Plus One.

55. Ermisch, J., 1995; 19.

56. Buck, N., and Scott, J., 1994, in Buck, N. et al, eds; 61.

57. Mattison, K., et al, 1994, *Remarriage and Stepfamilies*, Factsheet 7, One Plus One.

58. Haskey, J., 1994, *Population Trends* 78, OPCS, *General Household Survey*, 1993, and Brown, J.C., 1989, *Why Don't They Go to Work? Mothers on Benefit*, HMSO.

59. *Social Trends 25*, 1995. Figures also cited in Working Party report, Church of England's Board for Social Responsibility; 36 and 37.

60. This 'generation gap' in attitudes to single parents and in attitudes to the 'traditional' family has also been observed in our focus groups.

61. *Fiscal Studies*, 1993, Volume 14, No. 4, Institute of Fiscal Studies; 32.

62. As one might expect young non-working women still do more domestic labour because there is a stricter gender division of labour in the household.

63. The detailed breakdown of cooking, cleaning, washing and ironing comes from our analysis of Wave One of the British Household Panel Study. The figures are published here for the first time from a generational perspective. (see appendix)

64. Our *Socioconsult* analysis finds that attachment to the flexible family, which this question probes is strongly age related. Whilst our analysis shows that there is a lifestage effect, this does not negate the much stronger attachments that exist in this age range. The attachment index shows the following: 18-34 (1.10), 35-54 (0.87), 55+ (0.89).

65. Wellings, K., et al, 1994; 195.

66. Ahrendt, D., and Young, K., 1994 Chapter 7: 'Authoritarianism Updated'; 86. See also: Wellings, K., 1994.

67. Sullivan, A., 1995 *Virtually Normal*, (forthcoming), Picador. This covers a much broader gay rights agenda than that discussed here.

68. Henley Centre for Forecasting, 1994, Volume 1, Structural Change, 47.

69. *Social Trends 25* , 1995; 30.

70. Figures from the 1991 British Census, cited in Working Party, 1995, Church of England's Board for Social Responsibility; 40.

71. McGlone, F., and Cronin, N., 1994, *A Crisis in Care? The Future of Family and State Care for Older People in the European Union*, Occasional Paper 19, Family Policy Studies Centre; 31.

72. The number of single men between 30 and 44 is predicted to dramatically increase by 90 per cent between 1991 and 2001 and by 123 per cent between 1991 and 2011. The corresponding rates for women over the same periods are 65.5 per cent and 93.8 per cent whilst for the 20-29 year old age range, the next two decades are predicted to bring 10 per cent more bachelors and 12.3 per cent more spinsters. Department of Environment, 1995, 'Marital Status Projections', *Projections of the Households in England, 2016: 1992 based estimates of the numbers of households for regions, countries, metropolitan districts, and London boroughs*, Department of Environment

73. This has been confirmed in our qualitative research.

74. Lauer, R.H., Lauer, J.C., and Kerr, S.T., 1990, 'The Long-Term Marriage: Perceptions of Stability and Satisfaction', *International Journal of Aging and Human Development* , Volume 31; 189-195. See for example: Lauer, R.H., and Lauer, J.C., 1994, *Marriage and Family: The Quest for Intimacy*, Brown Communications Inc.

75. Argyle, M., 1987, *The Psychology of Happiness*; chapter 2, 'Social Relationships', Routledge.

76. Dormor, D.J., 1991, *Marriage and Partnership*, One Plus One.

77. Mattison, K., et al, 1994, *Impact of Divorce*, Factsheet 5, One Plus One. See also: Dominion, J., Mansfield, P., Dormor, D.J., and McAllister, F.,1991, *Marital Breakdown and the Health of the Nation: A Response to the Government's Consultative Document for Health in England*, One Plus One.

78. Dormor, D.J., 1991.

79. This is well documented in: Utting, D., 1995, *Family and Parenthood: Supporting Families, Preventing Breakdown*, Joseph Rowntree Foundation.

This provides a systematic and detailed analysis of research in this field. See also: Utting D., 1995, 'When the talking has to stop', *The Guardian*, 22 February and Cockett, M., Tripp, J., 1994, *Children Living in Reordered Families*, Social Policy Research Findings 45, Joseph Rowntree Foundation.

80. Walker, J., 1995, *The Cost of Communication Breakdown*, Relate Centre for Family Studies, Newcastle upon Tyne.

81. Mattison. K., et al, 1994, *Impact of Divorce*, Factsheet 5, One Plus One.

82. Utting, D., 1995, 'When the talking has to stop', *The Guardian* , 22 February and see also Utting, D., 1995.

83. Walker, J., 1995.

84. *Report of the All Party Parliamentary Group on Parenting and International Year of the Family UK, Parliamentary Hearings*, 1994, All Party Parliamentary Group on Parenting and International Year of the Family UK; 46. They also recommend some form of relationship education in schools.

85. Social and Community Planning Research, 1992, *British Social Attitudes: cumulative sourcebook: the first six surveys*, Gower, Aldershot and also, Ferri, E., ed, 1993 *Britain's 33 Year Olds - The fifth follow-up to the National Child Development Study*, ERSC and NCB.

86. Davis, G. and Murch, M., 1988, *Grounds for Divorce*, Clarendon Press, Oxford.

87. Walker, J., McCarthy, P., and Timms, N., 1994, *Mediation: The Making and Remaking of Cooperative Relationships - An Evaluation of the Effectiveness of Comprehensive Mediation*, University of Newcastle.

88. Kiernan, K. and Estaugh, V., 1993. This report includes a detailed analysis of the legal position of cohabitees relative to married couples.

89. See for example: Burns v Burns, 1984, 1 All ER 244 (the most frequently cited case in this respect) and Howard v Jones, 1989, *Family Law 231*, C.A. Kiernan, K., and Estaugh, V., 1993 give a detailed account of housing rights and the unmarried family. Parker, S., 1991, *Cohabitees*, 3rd ed, Longman, London. This book makes the point that in recent years the courts have begun to look more favourably on cases where contributions to household expenditure have enabled the other partner to meet the mortgage repayments.

90. Parker, S., 1991.

91. Kiernan, K., and Estaugh, V., 1993. See Chapter 5, 'Housing and the Unmarried Family'.

92. McRae, S., 1993; 106.

93. Law Commissioner, Charles Harpum, quoted in 'Review of the Property Rights of Non-Marital Cohabitants on the Breakup of Their

Relationship', 1994, *News From The Law Commission*, 11 May.

94. Ermisch, J., 1995.

95. McRae, S., 1993.

96. Ermisch, J., 1995.

97. Clarke, C., and Edmunds, R., 1992, *H v M: Equity and the Essex Cohabitant*, Family Law, December 1992. This case took place in 1992.

98. Morgan, P., 1995, *Farewell to the Family? Public Policy and Family Breakdown in Britain and the USA*, Choice in Welfare Series No. 21, IEA Health and Welfare Unit, London

99. McRae, S., 1993 .

100. Kiernan, K., and Estaugh, V., 1993. See Chapter 9, 'The European Experience'.

101. Everett, K., and Pawlowski, M., 1995, 'Transfer of Property Orders and Cohabitees', *Family Law*, August 1995. They argue that applying the principles of the South Wales Act would rectify the kind of anomalies highlighted in the Burns v Burns 1984 case.

102. *Towards Reform of the Law Relating to Cohabitation Outside Marriage*, 1987, Alberta Institute of Law Research and Reform; 59-60.

103. See for example the current terms of reference for the Law Commission's *Review of Property Rights of Non-Marital Cohabitants on The Break Up of Their Relationship*. Also, Clarke, L., and Edmunds, R., 1992 and, Burrows, D., 1995, 'Cohabitation - The Church Leads the Law', *Family Law*; 439.

104. McRae, S., 1993; 46.

105. Family Covenant Association, 1994; 49.

106. McRae, S., 1993; 106.

107. McRae, S., 1993 and Kiernan, K., and Estaugh, V., 1993.

108. This would not, of course, apply to single mothers who cannot or do not wish to identify the father.

109. It is possible for the second individual to become a guardian legally but the system is cumbersome and bureaucratic. Kiernan, K., and Estaugh, V., 1993. This book makes it clear that cohabiting couples do not have the legal right to adopt children.

110. Lord Michael Young of the Institute of Community Studies has campaigned for this for some time.

111. Johnson, P., and Falkingham, J., 1988, Intergenerational transfers and Public Expenditure on the Elderly in Modern Britain, *Ageing and Society*; 8.

112. Morgan, P., 1995.

113. Etzioni, A., 1994, *The Parenting Deficit*, Demos.

114. Hewitt, P., 1993, *About Time: The Revolution in Work and Family Life*, IPPR/Rivers Oram.

115. McRae, S., 1991, *Maternity Rights in Britain*, Policy Studies Institute.

116. The time squeeze, 1995, *Demos Quarterly* Issue 5, 1995; 7 and 23.

117. Hewitt, P., 1995, 'Whose Flexibility? Policies for Changing Times', *Demos Quarterly* Issue 5; 46. Hewitt argues that because many working mothers work part-time and because men work the longest hours in Europe, there is an equal opportunities deficit in the workplace and a fathering deficit at home.

118. Kraemer, S., 1995, *Active Fathering for the Future*, Working Paper 7, Demos. This includes a detailed analysis of attachment theory and the optimal conditions for good parenting.

119. Kraemer, S., 1995.

120. Lewis, C., and O'Brien, M. eds 1987, *Reassessing Fatherhood: New Observations on Fathers and the Modern Family*, London, Sage and see also Lee, C.,1993, *Talking tough and the fight for masculinity*, Harper Collins

121. *Working Nation: policies and programs*, 1994, Commonwealth of Australia

122. Duncan, A., Giles, C., and Webb, S., 1995, *The Impact of Subsidising Child Care*, Equal Opportunities Commission Discussion Series. This report provides a detailed cost/benefit analyses of the various child care options available.

123. British Market Research Bureau Survey for Age Concern, September 1990 and cited in: *Report of the All Party Parliamentary Group on Parenting and International Year of the Family UK Parliamentary Hearings;44.*

124. Crompton, R., 1994, *Paying the Price of Care: Women's employment and the Value of Caring*, Working Paper 4, Demos

125. *Families and Caring,* 1994, FactSheet 4, International Year of the Family.

126. Figures cited from evidence presented to the Commission on Social Justice by Melanie Henwood, in *Social Justice: Strategies for Social Renewal*, 1994, The Report of the Commission on Social Justice, IPPR; 84.

127. Walker, A., Alber, J., and Guillemard, A.M., 1993, *Older People in Europe: Social and Economic Policies*, The 1993 Report of the European Observatory on Older People, Commission of the European Communities.

128. McGlone, F., 1993; 27-33.

129. Dieck, M., 1994, 'Reforming Against the Grain: Long-Term Care in

Germany', *Social Policy Review* 6 , 1994, Social Policy Association. Historically family responsibilities have been clearly defined in German law which explicitly required children and parents to care for one another where necessary. Until 1994 social assistance was delivered by the municipalities and the states (Lander) when all other avenues of provision had been exhausted. These alternatives included using the private assets and income of family members to pay for care according to: Gotting, U., Haug, K., and Hinrichs, K., 1994, 'The Long Road to Long-Term Care Insurance in Germany', *Journal of Public Policy*, Volume 14, Part 3, Cambridge University Press; 285-309.

130. Alber, J., 1994, *Paying for Long Term Care in A Social Insurance System: The Example of Germany*, OECD. An estimated 11 per cent of the German population will reach 75 years and over in 2020. Germany in 1960 had a ratio of elderly people above the age of 75 to potential care givers in the 'daughter generation' (aged 45-69) of 1:5. In 1990 this had reduced to just 1:2. See Naegele, G., 1993, *ElderCare and the Workplace: A New Challenge for all Social Partners in Germany*, based on a paper presented to the British Institute of Gerontology. This cited evidence to show that younger generations of women balanced care demands with work and career potentials. See also: Federal Ministry of Labour and Social Affairs, 1994, *Social Security at a Glance*. According to this report, from 1995 it is estimated that 80 million German citizens will be covered by this scheme.

131. Demos is currently undertaking a study of long term care issues as part of its inter-generational politics project.

132. Dieck., M., 1994; 261.

133. McGlone, F., and Cronin, N., 1994; 31. This details changing care preferences.

134. Alber, J., 1994, *Paying for Long Term Care in A Social Insurance System: The Example of Germany*, OECD

135. Working Paper, 1995, Church of England's Board for Social Responsibility. This report was an attempt to come to terms with the changing nature of the family.

136. Bellos, A., 1995, 'Slump blamed for record divorces', *The Guardian*, 23rd August citing the 1995 Office of Population Censuses Report. 51 per cent of marriages are now civil.

137. A particularly eloquent case for gay marriage is provided by Sullivan, A. 1995 (forthcoming).

138. The Family Covenant Association, 1994, makes the case for these rituals. Lord Michael Young of the Family Covenant Association, has with Frank Field MP, been actively involved in promoting a Private Members Bill which will enable birth naming rituals to take place.

139. Morgan, P., 1995

140. Duncan, A., and Hobson, D., 1995, *Saturn's Children: How the State Devours Liberty, Prosperity and Virtue*, Sinclair-Stevenson, London.

Reconnecting politics

1. *Young People: Changing the Face of British Politics*, A Briefing by the British Youth Council, 1993.

2. John Curtice at the Department of Politics, University of Strathclyde calculates that as many as 45 per cent of people under 25 did not vote in the last election.

3. These figures are from *Youth and Politics*, an unpublished report prepared by the BBC Political Research Unit outlining the results of a poll conducted by NOP in December and January 1995 and reported on by the BBC.

4. This has been reinforced by the first phase of our qualitative research (see appendix). Our *Socioconsult* analysis reports similar findings. See also other research amongst ethnic minorities: Anwar , M., 1994, *Race and Elections: The Participation of Ethnic Minorities in Politics*, Centre for Research in Ethnic Relations, University of Warwick.

5. MORI/City and Guilds, 1995, *Teenager Aspiration Survey*

6. *What We are Concerned About; Youth Organisations in the Federal Republic of Germany*, 1992 German Youth Council.

7. *Le Monde*, 25 and 26 October 1994.

8. Cited in Eckersley, R., 1988, *The Casualties of Change: The Predicament of Youth in Australia*, Commission for the Future; 15.

9. Glasser, S., 1994 'Do Twentysomethings Hate Politics ?' *Who Cares* ; 22-23

10. Cited in Cohn, J. S., 1992, 'A Lost Political Generation', *The American Prospect*, no 9; 31-38

11. 'The Age of Indifference', 1990, a survey conducted by the Times-Mirror Center for Press and Politics and cited in Cohn, J. S., 1992; 33.

12. As many as 37 per cent of 18-21 year olds did not vote in 1984 and 29 per cent of those aged 22-29 did not vote in 1984. Volume 15, *Royal Commission on Electoral Reform and Party Financing*, Dundurn Press, Toronto; 40, table 2.4

13. *British Public Opinion* Newsletter,1995, Volume XVIII, No4, MORI reporting on the MORI/Joseph Rowntree Reform Trust 'State of the Nation' Survey.

14. Henley Centre for Forecasting, 1994, Volume 2:33

15. In the past six elections the government has had the support of less than a third of the electorate. The number of abstentions in general elections has also increased consistently from 16 per cent in 1950 to over 22 per cent in the 1992 election.

16. Riddell, P., 1994, 'Party Membership Plunges', *The Times*, 10 October.

17. 'Young Voters, Party People', 1995, *The Economist*, 26 August; 25. Ball, S., 1994, 'Vanishing Tories', *The Guardian*, 10 October puts the figure at 6,000 suggesting that there has been an increase of 1,500 since Autumn of last year.

18. Brown, C., 1995 'Cook claims pro Europe youth vote for Labour,' *The Independent*, 2 August. Previous research puts the average age of a Conservative member at 62. See: Richardson, J., Seyd, P., and Whiteley, P.,1994, *True Blues*, Clarendon Press, Oxford.

19. Duval Smith, A., 1994 'Ageing Tory Membership Threat to Funding', *The Guardian*, 10 October. See also: Richardson, J., Seyd, P., and Whiteley, P.,1994.

20. Duval-Smith, A., 1994 'Ageing Tory Membership threat to funding`, *The Guardian*, 10 October.

21. See Duval Smith, A., 'Ageing Tory Membership Threat to funding', *The Guardian*, 10 October 1994 and Seyd, P., and Whiteley, P., 1992, *Labour's Grass Roots, the Politics of Party Membership*, Clarendon Press, Oxford.

22. Cited in Waite, M., October 1994, 'The party with youth appeal ?', *Renewal*, Volume 2, No 4, 68

23. *Social Trends 25*, 1995, Central Statistical Office, HMSO; 74

24. See Frith, S., November 1981, 'Youth in the Eighties - A Dispossessed Generation', *Marxism Today*, London.

25. 'Young Voters: Party people', 1995, *The Economist* 26 August ; 25

26. Brown, C., 1995 'Cook claims pro Europe youth vote for Labour,' *The Independent*, 2 August.

27. *Social Trends 24*, CSO, 1994; 144

28. For further qualitative research on these and other women's organisations see Grant, J.,1995, *Where have all the women gone?: The experience of women aged between 18-34 in women's organisations*. Working Paper 6, Demos.

29. For more information see Wilkinson, H., 1994, Demos, and Siann, G., and Wilkinson, H.,1994, *Gender, Feminism and the Future*, Working Paper 3, Demos. Both reports detail widespread evidence of the extent of generational change and include the results of Demos' extensive qualitative research amongst women aged between 18-34 (see appendix)

30. Grant, J., 1995

31. Kelly and Breinlinger, 1995 (forthcoming), *Involvement in Women's Groups and Campaigns: Why Women Do or Don't Get Involved*, Birkbeck College, London University; 6

32. See ESRC Research briefing No. 4, 1992 *Careers and Identities: Adolescent Attitudes to Employment, Training and Education*. Bob Worcester, Chairman of MORI also provided Demos with details on environmental activism and links to age in 1994. This has been further confirmed by our own analysis of the *Socioconsult* survey.

33. These figures are from *Youth and Politics*, an unpublished report prepared by the BBC Political Research Unit outlining the results of a poll conducted by NOP in December and January 1995 and reported on by the BBC.

34. A MORI poll reported on in 'Who's Winning the Battle of the Sexes', *Mail on Sunday* 25 June 1995; 39 .

35. Bennie, L. G., and Rudig, W., 1993. 'Youth and the Environment - attitudes and actions in the 1990's', *Youth and Policy*, Issue 42, Houghton Le Spring. During the first phase of our qualitative research we found that there was considerably more interest shown in green politics than in party politics or women's politics and that this was the only area in which people had actually been active, but frequently in a low level way. See appendix for further details.

36. Grant, J., 1995; 14-15

37. *Youth and Politics*, report prepared by the BBC Political Research Unit, 1995.

38. See for example: Lowe, R., and Shaw, W., 1993, *Travellers - Voices of the new age nomads*, Fourth Estate, London.

39. See for example: Elliott, F., and Platt, S., 1993 'How can you sleep on Acid, anyway?', *New Statesman and Society*, London 16 July; 24-25.

40. There are several academic studies of new politics; see for example, Dalton, J., 1988, *Citizen Politics in Western Democracies: Public Opinion in the United States, Great Britain, West Germany and France*, Chatham House Publishers, New Jersey. Inglehart, R., and Rabier, J.R., 1986, 'Political Realignment in Advanced Industrial Society: From Class Based Politics to

Quality of Life Politics' *Government and Opposition*, 21; 456-479.

41. Halpern, D., 1995; 369-370.

42. Gallup, June 5 1995, cited in *British Public Opinion*, June newsletter, MORI; 12

43. See Ball, S., 1994, 'Vanishing Tories', *The Guardian*, 10 October and Ball, S. and Seldon, A., eds, 1994, *Conservative Century: The Conservative Party since 1900*, Oxford University Press.

44. Grant , J., 1995

45. See also: Henley Centre for Forecasting, 1994, and Ashford, S., and Timms, N. 1992, *What Europe thinks: A study of Western European values*, Aldershot, Dartmouth.

46. See Waite, M, 1994, *The Challenge of Youth; New Times*. This details trends in antisocial behaviour amongst today's young.

47. *Reforming Public Pensions*, 1988, OECD, Paris.

48. Walker, A., 1993, *Age and Attitudes, Main Results from a Eurobarometer Survey*, Commission of the European Communities; 3,4,4.

49. Cited in Walker, A., 1993 , 'Whither the Social Contract? Intergenerational Solidarity in Income and Employment', in Hobman, D., ed, 1993, *Uniting Generations: Studies in Conflicts and Co-operation*, Age Concern; 34.

50. *World Labour Report*, 1995, International Labour Organisation. This was also reported by Nicholas Timmins, 1995 'Ageing Population 'must work longer to fund pensions,' *The Independent*, 26 April.

51. See for example,Thompson, D., 'The Welfare State and Generation Conflict: Winners and Losers', in Johnson, P., et al, 1989, *Workers Versus Pensioners: Intergenerational Justice in an Ageing World*, Centre for Economic Policy Research, Manchester University Press; 33-56.

52. For poll details see: Etzioni, A., and Brodbeck, L., 1995, *The Intergenerational Covenant: Rights and Responsibilities, A Communitarian Working Paper*, The Communitarian Network, Washington; 21.

53. Grunwald, M., 1993, 'Making Their X', *The Boston Globe Magazine*, 28 November. See also J. P., 1993, 'Just Fix It', *US News and World Report*, February 22.

54. Grunwald, M., 1993; 19.

55. Rauch, J., 1995, 'Battle Stations' *The Economist*, 20 May; 56.

56. Daniel Callaghan's comments are cited in Etzioni A., and Brodbeck, L., 1995; 5. There is much dispute at the extent to which one can actually prove that there has been a policy shift away from young families and children to the elderly.

57. Johnson, P., and Falkingham, J., 1988; 129-146. The authors conclude that the relative declining position of younger generations is due to labour market conditions as opposed to welfare biases. Indeed, the authors conclude that the British welfare state has been remarkably fiscally neutral in its treatment of old and young.despite this they recognise that intergenerational equity issues are likely to become the focus of policy makers in Britain.

58. See 'Grey' Market and 'Youth' Market reports, Maps, January 1995. See also David Nicholson-Lord, 1995 "Greys' take over from the young as big spenders', *The Independent*, 27 January.

59. See Johnson, P., and Falkingham, J., 1988, and also Falkingham, J., and Victor, C., 1991, *The Myth of the Whoopie?: Incomes, The Elderly, and Targeting Welfare*, Welfare State programme, Working Paper, Number WSP/55. This focuses on the less well off elderley.

60. Henley Centre for Forecasting, 1994, Volume 2; 2-3

61. Walker, A., 1993, *Age and Attitudes;* 14.

62. James Meikle, 1995 'Student income falls as grant freeze bites', *The Guardian*, 29 March, reported that young people are running up average debts of well over £2,000 to cover the costs of university.

63. See Henley Centre for Forecasting, 1994, Volume 2; 24.

64. Hills, J., 1992, *Does Britain have a Welfare Generation? An Empirical Analysis of Intergenerational Equity*, Welfare State programme, Number WSP/76 and see also Falkingham, J., and Hills, J., 1995, *The Dynamic of Welfare: The Welfare State and the Lifecycle*, Harvester Wheatsheaf, 1995. Hills applies David Thomson's argument about a 'welfare generation' in New Zealand to Britain and concludes that the same analogy cannot be made. Each five year generation gets back at least 90 per cent of what it has put in. However, he also warns that the game only works so long as it is honoured and that any attempt to abolish or substantially scale down the welfare state would lead to younger generations losing heavily, having to invest for their own private provision as they continue to fund those who have not already done so. In addition if social security payments continued to be price rather than income-linked over the next fifty years, the picture would deteriorate for those born after 1921.

65. The Rt. Hon. Peter Lilley MP, Secretary of State for Social Security recently interviewed on Radio 4's Analysis programme commented that ..." It (the government) ought to encourage people to make their own provision, both for themselves and for future generations as they see fit, obviously for themselves and their families. Then that means that any burdens that fall on the state in this generation or in the future will be minimal." Transcript of 'What's Posterity Done for Me?', *Analysis*, Radio 4, 20 June; 8-9.

66. For an example of this thinking see: Walker, A., in Hobman, D., ed, 1993, Hills, J., 1992 and Falkingham. J., and Hills, J., 1995.

67. Walker, A., 1993, *Age and Attitudes*; 15-20.

68. MERIC, 1994. For further information on Global Generation X see: Samms, C., 1995, Working Paper 8.

69. Walker, A., 1993, *Age and Attitudes*; 20

70. For an example of a more imaginative scheme for funding old age pensions see the proposals made in Field, F., MP, 1995, *Making Welfare Work: Reconstructing Welfare for the Millennium*, Institute of Community Studies.

71. See Lean democracy, 1994, *Demos Quarterly* Issue 3, Demos, for a range of detailed proposals in this area.

72. This is recommended in Mulgan, G., and Wilkinson, H., 1994, *Demos Quarterly* Issue 5 and in Stewart, J., 1995, *Innovation in Democratic Practice*, Institute of Local Government Studies, University of Birmingham.

73. Stewart, J. 1995; 33. Placing polling stations near local shops have been known to improve turnout.

74. *Report of the working party on electoral systems*, 1993, Labour Party.

75. Stewart, J, 1995; 33.

76. *Australian Electoral Commission Annual Report*, 1993-94; 33

77. Confirmed in writing by the Australian Electoral Commission, (AEC) 1995. See also *Identifying Barriers and Motivators for 'Enrolment' for young people*, 1989 a report by Elliott and Shanahan Research for the AEC, Sydney; 12-13.

78. *Strategy for A Comprehensive National Voter Education Program*, 1994, Elections Canada.

79. MORI, 1995, *State of the Nation;* 7-8

80. In our latest focus groups we have found a particularly high rate of ignorance amongst unemployed 18-25 year old men.

81. See Elliott and Shanahan, 1989; 13. See also: Phillips, A., 1991 'Citizen Who, Citizen How ?', *RSA Journal*, Vol 139; 515-523.

82. *Looking to the Future: Towards a Coherent Youth Policy*, 1993, British Youth Council: 21. This recommended that 'Education for Citizenship' should be introduced as a core part of the National Curriculum.

83. The Australian Electoral Commission is a statutory authority responsible for conducting federal and other elections and referendums, maintaining the electoral roll and conducting electoral education. In Canada, the Office of the Chief Elections Officer of Canada, (also known as Elections Canada) performs the same functions.

84. *Report of the Working Party on Electoral Systems*, 1993, Labour Party; 40

85. Elliott and Shanahan Research, 1989.

86. 'Survey on Australian Electoral Roll', the Roy Morgan Research Centre Pty. Ltd., 1987, cited in Elliott and Shanahan, 1989; 9

87. Confirmed in writing by the Australian Electoral Commission 1995

88. *Report of the Working Party on Electoral Systems*, 1993, Labour Party;41

89. *Campaigns and Elections*, July 1995.

90. Star, A.,1993,'The TwentySomething Myth', *The New Republic* January 10 & 11. The author makes the point that it is important to emphasise that Clinton's slice of the 18-29 year old vote was no larger than his share of the total popular vote and that although 50 per cent of 18-24 year olds were unregistered, it was the turnout of registered young voters that dropped fastest in the 1980s.

91. 'Young Voters, Party People' 1995, *The Economist*, August 26; 24

92. Glasser, S. B., 1994, 'Do Twentysomethings Hate Politics ?` *Who Cares?*; 24. The same principles could be extended to many other places where young people are found in greater numbers.

93. Glasser, S.B., 1994; 25.

94. From a draft paper outlining The Ministry of Sound's project.

95. Star, A., 1993 'The Twentysomething Myth', *The New Republic*, 4 and 11 January; 23

96. Votes at 16 are now on the agenda in Canada and Australia.

97. MORI, 1995, *The State of the Nation*; 73 per cent of 18-34 year olds support a bill of rights, although different generations disagree about exactly what it should include. For example, 68 per cent of 18-34 year olds think it should include the right of those who are homeless to be housed, compared with 51 per cent of over 55s; 66 per cent of young people would include the right of a woman to have an abortion, compared with 51 per cent of over 55 year olds.

98. Conversations with Carole Croche of Australian Youth Political Action Committee (AYPAC), Clive Bean of Australia National University and Steven Crook, University of Tasmania, August 1995.

99. Conversation with Elizabeth Thurbon, Australian Electoral Commission, August 1995 and also Ian McAllister, the Australian expert on compulsory voting.

100. McAllister, I., 1986 'Electoral Turnout and Party Advantage in

Australia,'*Politics*; 89-93

101. According to a poll cited in McAllister, I., 1986; 89.

102. According to research in Elliott and Shanahan, 1989; 23

103. Conversation with AYPAC personnel, August 1995.

104. For a detailed argument putting the case for generational accounting see: Kotlikoff, L. J., 1992, *Generational Accounting: Knowing Who Pays, and When, for What We Spend*, Free Press, New York.

105. Walker, A., 1993, in Hobman, D., ed; 34. Briscoe, I., 1995, Time rights in the 1990s: An international survey, *Demos.Quarterly* Issue 5; Demos 37-38.

106. This quote is from the Minister's speech and has been supplied to us by the Ministry's press office. The first two briefs of the Ministry of Solidarity for Generations were to consider child care demands and the needs of elderly dependents.

107. Demos will be undertaking a comprehensive study of inter-generational politics in the near future which will expand on these themes and draw lessons from abroad.

Bibliography

Alber, J., 1994, *Paying for Long Term Care in a Social Insurance System; The Example of Germany*, OECD.

Anwar, M., 1994, *Race and Elections: The Participation of Ethnic Minorities in Politics*, Centre for Research in Ethnic Relations, University of Warwick.

Argyle, M., 1987, *The Psychology of Happiness*, Routledge.

Ashford, S. and Timms, N.,1992, *What Europe thinks: A study of Western European values*, Aldershot, Dartmouth.

Ball, S., and Seldon , A., eds,1994 *Conservative Century: the Conservative Party Since 1900*, Oxford University Press.

Barclay, Sir P., 1995, *Joseph Rowntree Foundation Inquiry into Income and Wealth*, Volume 1, Joseph Rowntree Foundation.

Bridges, W., 1995, *Job Shift:How to Prosper in a World Without Jobs*, Allen and Unwin.

British social attitudes, the 11th report, 1994, Dartmouth Publishing, Aldershot.

British social attitudes, the 8th report, 1991, Dartmouth Publishing, Aldershot.

British Social Attitudes:cumulative sourcebook:the first six surveys, 1992, Gower

Buck, N., Gershuny, J., Rose, D.,Scott, J., 1994, *Changing Households: The British Household Panel Survey 1990-92*, ESRC Research Centre on Micro-Social Change.

Dalton, R. J., 1988, *Citizen Politics in Western Democracies: Public Opinion in the United States, Great Britain, West Germany and France*, Chatham House Publishers, New Jersey.

Davis, G., and Murch, M., 1988, *Grounds for Divorce*, Clarendon Press, Oxford.

Department of Environment, 1995, *Projections of the Households in*

England,2016, London.

Dormor, D. J., 1992, *The Relationship Revolution: Cohabitation, Marriage and Divorce in Contemporary Europe*, One Plus One.

Duncan, A., Giles, C., and Webb, S., 1995, *The Impact of Subsidising Child Care*, Equal Opportunities Commission Discussion Series, Manchester.

Duncan, A., and Hobson, D., 1994, *A Crisis in Care ? The Future of Family and State Care for Older People in the European Union*, Occasional Paper 19, Family Policy Study Centre, London

Eckersley, R., 1988, *The Casualties of Change: The Predicament,of Youth in Australia*, Commission for the Future, Dickson, ACT.

Ermisch, J., 1995, *Premarital Cohabitation, Childbearing and the Creation of One Parent Families*, Working Paper 15-17, ESRC Research Centre on Micro-Social Change, Essex.

Etzioni, A., and Brodbeck, L., 1995, *The Intergenerational Covenant: Rights and Responsibilities, A Communitarian Working Paper*, The Communitarian Network, Washington.

Falkingham, J., and Hills, J., 1995, *The Dynamic of Welfare: The Welfare State and the Lifecycle*, Harvester Wheatsheaf.

Falkingham, J., and Victor, C., 1991, *The Myth of the Whoopie? Incomes, the Elderly and Targetting Welfare*, Welfare State Programme, Working Paper No. WSP/55, London School of Economics.

Field, F., MP, 1995, *Making Welfare Work: Reconstructing Welfare for the Millennium*, Institute of Community Studies, London

Finlayson, P., Reynolds, I., Rob, M., Muir, C., 1987, *Adolescents - their views, problems and needs*, The Hornsby Ku Ring Gai Area Health Service, Australia.

Freedman, M., *Seniors in National and Community Service: A Report Prepared for the Commonwealth Fund's Over 55 At Work Program*, Public/Private Ventures, Philadelphia.

Fukuyama, F., 1995, *Trust: The Social Virtues and Creation of Prosperity*, Hamish Hamilton, London.

Gillis, J., R., 1985, *For Better or Worse: British Marriages 1600 to the Present*, Oxford University Press.

Harkness, S., and Machin, S., 1995 (forthcoming) *Changes in Women's Wages in Britain: What has Happened to the Male/Female Wage Differential Since the mid 1970's?*, Centre for Economic Performance, London School of Economics.

Harkness, S. and Waldfogel, J., 1995, *Evaluating the Pin Money Hypothesis: The Relationship Between Women's Labour Market Activity, Family Income and Poverty in Britain*, Discussion Paper No. WP/108, Welfare State Programme, Centre for Economic Performance, London School of Economics.

Henley Centre for Forecasting, 1994, *Planning for Social Change*, Volume 1, Structural Trends and Volume 2, Analysis and Implications.

Herriot, P., and Pemberton, C., 1995, *New Deals:The Revolution in Managerial Careers*, John Wiley and Sons.

Hills, J., 1992, *Does Britain Have a Welfare Generation? An Empirical Analysis of Intergenerational Equity?*,Welfare State Programme, No. WP/76, London

School of Economics.

Hills J., 1995, *Joseph Rowntree Foundation Inquiry into Income and Wealth*, Vol.II, Joseph Rowntree Foundation.

Hobman, D., ed, 1993, *Uniting Generations: Studies in Conflicts and Co-operation*, Age Concern, London.

How to Make A Family Covenant: Child Welcoming Ceremonies, 1994, The Family Covenant Association.

Inglehart, R.,1977, *The Silent Revolution: Changing values and political styles among Western publics*, Princeton.

Inglehart, R., 1990, *Culture Shift in Advanced Industrial Society*, Princeton.

Johnson, P., Conrad, C., and Thomson, D., eds, 1989, *Workers Versus Pensioners: Intergenerational Justice in an Ageing World*, Centre for Economic Policy Research, Manchester University Press.

Joshi, H., Paci, P., 1995 (forthcoming)) *Wage differentials between men and women*, Department of Employment, London.

Kandola, R., and Fullerton, J., 1994, *Managing the Mosaic:Diversity in Action*, Institute of Personnel and Development, London.

Kiernan, K., E., and Estaugh, V., 1993, *Cohabitation: Extra Marital ChildBearing and Social Policy*, Occasional Paper, Family Policy Studies Centre, London

Kotlikoff, L.J., 1992, *Generational Accounting : Knowing Who Pays and When, for What We Spend*, Free Press, New York.

Lauer, R., H., and Lauer, J., C., 1994, *Marriage and Family: The Quest for Intimacy*, Brown Communications Inc

Leach, P., 1994, Children First: *What Society Must Do - And Is Not Doing - For Children Today*, Penguin.

Lean democracy, 1994, *Demos Quarterly* Issue 3, Demos.

Lee, C., 1993, *Talking Tough and the fight for masculinity*, Harper Collins

Lewis, C., and O'Brien, M., eds, 1987, *Reassessing Fatherhood:New Observations on Fathers and the Modern Family*, Sage, London.

Lewis, J., Clark, D., Morgan, D., 1992, *Whom God Hath Joined Together*, Routledge, London.

Liberation Technology, 1994, *Demos Quarterly*, Issue 4, Demos.

Lindley, R., ed, 1994, *Labour Market Structures and Prospects for Women*, Research Series, Equal Opportunities Commission, Manchester

Looking to the Future: Towards A Coherent Youth Policy, 1993, British Youth Council, London

Lowe, R., and Shaw, W., 1993, *Travellers - Voices of the new age nomads*, Fourth Estate, London.

Machin, S., and Waldfogel, J., 1994, *The Decline of the Male Breadwinner: Changing Shares of Husbands' and Wives' Earnings in Family Income*, WSP/103, Welfare State Programme, London School of Economics.

Marmor, T.R., et al, eds, 1994, *Economic Security and Intergenerational Justice - A Look at North America,* The Urban Institute.

Mattison, K., McAllister, F., and Roberts, K., 1994, *One Plus One Information Pack,* One Plus One, London.

McGlone, F., and Cronin, N., 1994, *A Crisis in Care: The Future of Family and State Care for Older People in the European Union*, Occasional Paper 19,

Family Policy Studies Centre, London.

McRae, S., 1991, *Maternity Rights in Britain*, Policy Studies Institute, London.

McRae, S., 1993, *Cohabiting Mothers: Changing Marriage and Motherhood?* Policy Studies Institute, London.

Megyery, K., ed, 1991, *Youth in Canadian Politics, Participation and Involvement, Royal Commission on Electoral Reform and Party Financing* Vol. 8, Dundurn Press, Toronto.

Modood, T., Beishon, S., and Virdee, S., 1994, *Changing Ethnic Identities*, Policy Studies Institute, London.

Morgan, P., 1995, *Farewell to the Family? Public Policy and Family Breakdown in Britain and the USA*, Choice in Welfare Series No. 21, IEA Health and Welfare Unit, London.

Mulgan, G.,1994, *Politics in an Anti-Political Age*, Polity Press, Cambridge.

Parker, S., *Cohabitees*, Longman, 3rd ed.

Plummer, J.,1994, *The Governance Gap: Quangos and Accountability*, Joseph Rowntree Foundation in association with Demos.

Reforming Public Pensions, 1988, OECD, Paris.

Richardson, J., Seyd, P, and Whiteley, P., 1994, *True Blues*, Clarendon Press, Oxford.

Robinson, P., 1995, *Qualifications and the Labour Market: Do the National Education and Training Targets Make Sense?* Discussion Paper WP No. 736, London School of Economics

Royal Commission on Electoral Reform and Party Financing , Volume 15, Dundurn Press, Toronto.

Rutter, M., and Smith, J., eds, 1995, *Psychosocial Disorders in Young People: Time Trends and their Causes,* John Wiley and Sons, Chichester.

Sampson, A., 1995, *Company Man:The Rise and Fall of Corporate Life*, Harper Collins, London.

Seyd, P., and Whiteley, P.,1992, *Labour's Grass Roots The Politics of Party Membership.* Clarendon Press, Oxford.

Social Focus on Women, 1995, Central Statistical Office, London.

Social Trends 24 , 1994, Central Statistical Office, London.

Social Trends 25, 1995, Central Statistical Office, London.

Something to Celebrate: Valuing Families in Church and Society, 1995, Working Party report, Church of England's Board for Social Responsibility, Church House Publishing, London.

Stewart, J., 1995, *Innovation in Democratic Practice*, Institute of Local Government Studies, University of Birmingham.

Sullivan, A., 1995 (forthcoming), *Virtually Normal*, Picador Press.

The end of unemployment: bringing work to life, 1994, *Demos Quarterly* Issue 2, Demos.

Utting, D., 1995, *Family and Parenthood:Supporting Families and Preventing Breakdown*, Joseph Rowntree Foundation.

Viney, J., and Osborne, J.,1995, *Modernising Public Appointments*, Demos.

Waldfogel, J., 1993, *Women Working for Less: A Longitudinal Analysis of the Family Gap*, Discussion Paper No. WSP/93, Welfare State Programme, Centre for Economic Performance, London School of Economics.

Walker, A., 1993, *Age and Attitudes, Main Results from a Eurobarometer Survey*, Commission of the European Communities..

Walker, A., Alber, J., and Guillemard, A-.M., 1993, *Older people in Europe: Social and Economic Policies*. Commission of the European Communities.

Walker, J., 1995, *The Cost of Communication Breakdown*, Relate Centre for Family Studies, Newcastle Upon Tyne.

Wellings, K., Field, J., Johnson, A.M., and Wadsworth, J., 1994, *Sexual Behaviour in Britain: The National Survey of Sexual Attitudes and Lifestyles*, Penguin Books, London.

Wilkinson, H., 1994, *No turning back: generations and the genderquake*, Demos, London.

World Labour Report,1995, International Labour Organisation.

Appendix

The research for this book was carried out in two stages; the first stage involved qualitative research into attitudes on a range of issues concerning work, politics and relationships, and the second stage provided quantitative data on the same areas.

Qualitative Research

The fieldwork took place in three phases:

Phase One:

Qualitative research amongst representative samples of women and men aged between 18-34. This was commissioned and managed by Demos and conducted by Opinion Leader Research. It took the form of a combination of group discussions and depth interviews. There were eight focus groups amongst women and four amongst men. These groups spanned the range of class, age and marital and employment status, and they took place in the North, the South and the Midlands. The sample was boosted to include some ethnic minority depth interviews and particular sub groups within the age group such as single parents (male and female) and young families 12 depth interviews were conducted in total.

This research has been published as part of the working paper series. For a more detailed appendix contact Demos.

Phase Two:

Qualitative research amongst workers in three different sectors of the economy. This was conducted in house by the Demos research team. All in all 19 group discussions took place around the country amongst professionals, journalists and factory workers. There were 13 with young professionals (ABs) with seven groups of women and six amongst men. 6 groups took place with unskilled uneducated workers (C2Ds): 2 groups of women, 2 of men, one mixed group and a group of Asian women. These casestudies have been published as working papers.

Phase Three:

Qualitative research amongst six groups of white unemployed men aged between 18-24 as part of Demos' ongoing young men project. The groups took place in rural as well as urban areas and were with unemployed men with few or no qualifications. These group discussions will be complemented in the near future by groups amongst ethnic minority males and will be published in the coming months.

Quantitative Research

British Household Panel Study, ESRC Research Centre on Micro-Social Change, Essex University. The BHPS is an annual household panel survey of approximately 10,000 respondents and aims to interview, over a number of years, all members of a household where sample members are resident. The study has currently completed four waves of interviews although Wave Four is currently being 'cleaned' up before it can be analysed with confidence. The Wave 3 data set, conducted in September 1993, is the most up to date survey available for analysis and is the major source for this report. The scale of the sample makes it possible to analyse in some detail the differences between various groups. To shed further light on the division of domestic responsibilities between women and men and between the generations we also used data from Wave One (which was carried out in September 1991) for the age range under consideration and used it to examine patterns of behaviour with respect to cooking, cleaning, washing, ironing, and child care responsibilities. All data is published here for the first time.

MORI Socioconsult's most up to date survey was analysed for the 18-34 generation, for sub-groups within the generation (for example, broken down by class and lifestage) and across the generations to conduct comparisons. This was the first time that this database had been analysed with these issues in mind. The data is drawn from a study conducted in September 1994, in which 2,143 adults (15+) provided information about their values and their attitudes on a wide range of issues including technological change, politics, the environment, work, and family and social relationships. The sample was representative of the population of Great Britain and was conducted at 225 sampling points. In our interpretation of the data we have also been able to call upon information about socio-cultural change in other European countries, the USA and Canada from the *Socioconsult International Network*.

For further information about methodology please contact Demos.